MONEY, MOTIVATION, and MISSION IN THE SMALL CHURCH

MONEY, MOTIVATION, and MISSION IN THE SMALL CHURCH

ANTHONY PAPPAS

DOUGLAS ALAN WALRATH
GENERAL EDITOR

Judson Press® Valley Forge

Library of Congress Cataloging-in-Publication Data

Pappas, Anthony.
     Money, motivation, and mission in the small church.

     (Small church in action)
     Bibliography: p.
     1. Small churches. 2. Church finance. I. Walrath,
     Douglas Alan, 1933- . II. Title. III. Series.
     BV637.8.P37   1989   254.8   88.34778
     ISBN 0-8170-1146-3

A special thanks
to three people who saw, or thought they saw,
writer's potential in me:
    Don Crosby, Floyd Miller, and Paul Gillespie;
to Doug Walrath for shepherding this book into existence;
and especially to the people at The Harbor Church,
    Block Island,
and particularly Brad, who didn't know it couldn't be done!

Contents

1

Stewardship in the Small Church

Commitment and Struggle

Commitment

All healthy giving to the cause of Christ is based on commitment. But not all commitment is the same. Much of the literature on stewardship assumes that Christians are motivated to give in order to accomplish something. This is especially the case in large, program-oriented churches. In these churches more giving translates directly into more ministry. Those Christians who are committed to seeing the kingdom of God become more real in their midst are motivated to give and to give more. But some Christians are committed not so much to the work of Christ as to their familial relationship with Christ. These Christians understand their commitment as more to well-being than to well-doing. Interestingly, one tends to find a much higher percentage of this type of Christian in the small church!

The church of my youth and the church that I now pastor— both small churches—offer insight into this distinction in stewardship motivation. The small church I grew up in emphasized being born again, tithing (at least), and living a sanctified life. But I don't remember clearly in what order. One of my earliest recollections of that church was of being trapped behind my rather outspoken mother in the line to shake the pastor's hand

after yet another long-winded and financially oriented sermon. "Can't you think of another topic to preach on?" she
asked him. "After all, there is more to being a Christian than
tithes and offerings. We're already giving all we can. What do
you want, blood from a turnip?" Apparently he got blood
from the other turnips because, though a working-class congregation, they gave at a very high per capita level. Their
annual contributions to mission exceeded the monies spent in
maintaining the church building and the pastor! In looking
back on that congregation, I think the giving was so significant
because each person was concerned with his or her own well-
being. And the congregation saw a major connection between
tithing and their spiritual health. Not smoking, not drinking,
coming to Wednesday night prayer meetings, and tithing were
significant signs to an individual (and others) that, indeed, "I
am right with God; my spiritual well-being is assured."

My spiritual journey has taken me down many roads since
that congregation of my youth, and I now find myself the pastor of another small church. This congregation emphasizes the
love of God, the joy of Christian fellowship, and the fulfillment of service. Tithing, although encouraged, is still a minor-
ity activity. But what is not in question is a commitment to the
well-being of the parish. When we head into December well in
the financial hole, a swollen Christmas offering carries us into
the black. When a unique opportunity to pave our church
driveway occurred (there are no asphalt plants on our island),
an afternoon on the phone netted our trustee chair enough
funds to get the job done on the spot. When our century-old
windows and half-century-old furnace decided to retire
together, our parish members, members of the community,
and seasonal friends dug in and pulled the church through.
When we were looking at five thousand dollars in loan payments, a group of men built picnic tables, another group spent
all day up to their elbows in chicken fat, another manned a
barbecue pit, another boiled corn, another served delicious
meals, another cleaned up an enormous mess. The well-being
of the congregation was at stake. We might use chicken instead

of tithing, but when our well-being is at stake we respond.

It is interesting to note that neither the parish in which I grew up nor the one in which I currently pastor nor any other small church of which I am aware responds well to "well-doing." Well-doing seems not only not to motivate but actually to "de-motivate" small church people. This is so for two reasons.

The first is that the per capita effort in small churches is already larger than in large churches. People in small churches are already doing more. They do more to keep the doors open and the church clean. Per person they do more Sunday School teaching, more "hat wearing," more filling in of the cracks. And because they are individually more vital to the church than individual large church members, they feel a sense of responsibility that, in all honesty, can itself be tiring! The call to give more in order to do more is akin to attempting to per-suade a bedouin to buy a truckload of sand. Of that we have more than enough, thank you.

But the reason an appeal to give more based on doing more is de-motivational in a small church runs deeper than fatigue. It basically misunderstands the nature of the small church. Although a committed small church member does more, this is not what counts in his or her value framework. A parent cer-tainly does more than a baby-sitter for the well-being of the child, but the level of activity is not the essence of parenthood. The loving relationship that results in a sense of identity between the parent and the child motivates and undergirds the level of doing. Parents give more because they love their child and find fulfillment in the health of their relationship. Just so, the small church members are motivated to preserve or enhance the well-being of their church because they find in that context what is most meaningful in their lives.

I am intrigued at how seldom the literature on motivating giving in the church takes this fundamental truth of the small church into account. On the contrary, if I had a nickel for each stewardship piece I have encountered that instructed me to motivate my people to give more by presenting to them a pic-ture of what the church could DO if they would only give

more, my church could retire its debt! Some people are motivated by calls to action. Some churches are energized by programmatic challenges. By and large, though, these churches
are mid- and large-sized, are located in suburban and urban
settings, lodge their identity in their activity, and are bureaucratic in structure. God bless these churches.

But what about my church and your church? What about
the church that is too small to run major programs? What
about the church that knows itself in relationships, not in
actions? What about the church that bumbles around learning
how to do something, and when it finally learns how to do it
right, is so proud of itself that it keeps on doing that activity
for years because it has become ingrained in that process?
What about the church that is structured not around programs, but around persons? In such churches the appeal to
give more in order to do more is about as effective as shoveling
sand against the tide. In such churches the appeal must be to
well-being not to well-doing. It may be the sense of well-being
of the individual's commitment to Christ, or (and I think this is
more common in small churches) it may be the well-being of
the whole group.

One of the realities that strengthens well-being is struggling!
We would all like life to be easy, but the struggle is God's classroom. Maybe the greatest struggle that the small church faces
is the financial one. Can any good come out of this struggle?
Let us briefly consider my parish's experience before we
explore this question more deeply in the next chapter.

Struggle

Atlas claimed he could move the world if he had a place to
stand. Where one stands is critical in relation to what one
intends to move. I have read too many books penned by those
who would move the small church but who stood squarely
outside of the small church. I am writing this book to small
churches from the inside. I have been a small church person all
my life and have pastored a small church on Block Island for
more than a dozen years. I love my parish. Its strengths sustain

me. Its weaknesses hurt me. We commit ourselves to keep our church afloat because truly it is a ship of life in a sea of materialism, hedonism, and anonymity. We've kept the doors open in "lean" years, and we have painted them in "fat" years. Regarding small church finances, I don't know all the answers—maybe not even any. But I know that keeping the small church afloat is one challenge worth wrestling with.

Keeping the small church going is a struggle. Our congregation has struggled from even before its beginning. In 1659 the elders of Massachusetts Bay Colony condemned to death Mary Dyer for the crime of publicly sharing her religious beliefs. In the shadow of the gallows upon which she was hung, sixteen men of Boston met behind closed doors to formulate plans to sell all their holdings and move to a place where they could worship God by their own light. They chose to settle harborless Block Island and struggled to overcome the hostility of the native people. They struggled against nature, clearing fields, felling trees, building houses, constructing ships. They struggled to keep their faith alive, going almost a century and a half without being able to depend on the presence of educated and ordained clergy. They struggled on, ministered to by three dedicated laymen, God raising one up for three successive generations. On the eve of the Revolution, they struggled to build a church building and become formally organized as a church. They struggled to find their common faith and stay unified as the body of Christ.

They struggled on against "acts of God." In fact, in that struggle they found the hand of God. Over the course of the last two and a quarter centuries, four church buildings have burned to the ground. Each time the congregation was plunged into a crisis. Give up or rebuild? Rebuild on the same site or elsewhere? Each time the crisis occasioned recommitment— commitment to God—for each time the congregation gathered the resources to rebuild. And commitment to ministry—for each time the church was rebuilt in a different location. Over the centuries, the social, civic, and commercial "center" of the island has shifted. The initial settlement was in a protected vale in the southern portion of the island. Later the grist mill, town hall, and shops were built at a spot midway between the east and west coasts. Then, toward the end of the nineteenth century, a permanent harbor was constructed on the east coast. Immediately the economic and social life of the community became concentrated adjacent to this harbor. Each time that the church was rebuilt, it was rebuilt in the new center of the community. The geography bespoke the congregation's vision of ministry: to be present to the center of the community's life.

And they struggled against "acts of man." The proximity of the island to Newport, Rhode Island, gave the island an unprecedented economic boom during the Gay Nineties. This expansive lifestyle was soon dashed by the pendulum's return swing. The Great Depression and the Second World War (and a devastating hurricane in 1938) brought the island's economy to its knees. The population diminished to a quarter of its size during the early decades of this century. The island was reduced to a few hundred stubborn, impoverished, elderly Yankees. The church struggled to keep its doors open. Many people remember when ten at worship on Sunday morning was a goodly number. The belt was tightened. Retired pastors were paid with a roof and a pittance. Little-used portions of the church building were cannibalized to repair the main sections. The sanctuary was abandoned for the winter. Sunday School lapsed. Only the iron rule of the treasurer kept the bills at a payable level.

And they struggled to keep their vision alive. "Retired" pastor Rev. W. Stanley Pratt determined to be the end of the era of just hanging on, so he worked with the people to build up the ministry and undergird their vision. The Sunday School was restarted, fund-raisers initiated, new bylaws adopted. Shoots of new life were appearing. Upon Stan's retirement, the church determined to call a young, full-time pastor. It was, as they later described it, a "step of faith." (Had I realized at the time how precarious my paycheck really was, I would have been frightened into immobility. But being blissfully ignorant, I proceeded as if we weren't "marginal," and pretty soon we became "viable!") So I was called in 1976 to be the first full-time pastor of the First Baptist Church of Block Island (the Harbor Church) in a number of decades. Through the grace of God, the love and patience of the parishioners, sheer dumb luck, and my ability to see the handwriting on the wall seconds before I crashed into it, the vision of the people has been vindicated.

And we continue to struggle. Our budget has grown from one year to the next, due to inflation, increased ministry, and getting around to paying for services rendered. Most years we meet our expenses (if not the budget), but it is always touch and go at the end of the year. (Christmas, with its offering, could not come at a better time!) We determined to do two decades worth of repairs on the building before it was too late. It took us five years, but we raised the monies. For these are the "fat" years in which we move ahead, knowing that lean years will follow. But even so we struggle. Our capital fund drive fell $35,000 short, requiring $5330 in annual payments. Our new treasurer has already told me privately there is no way we will meet our expenses this year. Prophet of doom or realist? Only time will tell. (Actually, I'm glad of his position. Small church treasurers should not be Pollyannas. It makes the rest of us too comfortable.)

This history shows certain things. It shows, first of all, that life is struggle. One of the reasons I share my own parish's history is that we are one of the oldest worshiping congregations in the country. From our conception in Massachusetts and our inception on Block Island, hardly without exception for three and a quarter centuries, our life has been struggle. There have been, I am told, some brief periods when life flowed smoothly, productively, and with little effort. But these periods are hardly the rule. The rule is blood, sweat, and tears, sacrifice and work, vision and hope, and waiting thirty-eight years (as the man mentioned in John 5:2-9) for the waters to be troubled. The rule is toughing out the lean years, keeping the doors open so that when the Spirit of God chooses to move, there will be at least a point of beginning. Life in the small church is struggle.

A struggle of faith. A struggle of fellowship. A struggle of fidelity. A struggle of finances. Thus it is. And I have gone back a third of a millenium to show that thus it has always been. In the small church, life is struggle.

But struggle is also life. My parish may have struggled for three-hundred plus years, but it has been around for three-hundred years to struggle. Life may have been a struggle for my parishioners and their forebears, but in that struggle God gave them life. The point is they were not overcome by their struggles, but they remained faithful, persevering as best they could, and God's Spirit vindicated their efforts. But more than this, the struggles were also God's tools for growth and righteousness. The struggle to rebuild after the church was destroyed by fire was in fact God's call to continue to minister at the center of community life. The failure to obtain a clergyman brought forth the best in laymen such as Simon Ray and Thomas Dodge. Struggle is life. Somehow God gives the power to remain steadfast in the struggle. And more than this—God uses our struggles as a means of growth for us.

It is on the basis of this struggle that I presume to write a book on keeping the small church afloat financially. I write from the history of the struggles of my parish to the story of the struggle of your parish. The history of the struggle of my parish—its sacrifice and faithfulness—calls me to struggle today. And I call you to face your struggle—for that is the heritage on which you stand. The particulars in your parish will vary, but the theme is the same: a vision of God's purpose in our midst, sacrifice and struggle toward that end, and the Spirit of the living God quickening our efforts.

What This Book Is Not About

This is not a book on tithing. Tithing is great. It is biblical and practical. I have tithed since I earned my first dime. I'm all for it. But there are many good books on tithing. This isn't one of them.

It isn't a new (or dusted off) program to make your small church's financial drives successful. I have no surefire gimmicks guaranteed to solve all your problems. There is no one solution—there is only the ongoing struggle. However, at some points I will refer to certain stewardship ideas that I think typify an approach I believe to be faithful and worthwhile in the small church.

This is not a book on adapting larger church stewardship approaches or business fund-raising strategies to the small church. If this is what you want, may I suggest that you go back to John 3:16 and start your Christian life all over again.

This is not a book filled with magic or instant solutions to your financial struggles. Rather, it is a book that will better equip you for the struggle and help you to undergird yourselves and to realize that you are in it for the long run.

This is not one of those "I did it, so there is no reason why you can't, too" books. Certainly we can learn from one another various helpful attitudes and approaches to raising funds. But I would not presume to write a book whose message is: by being faithful in my setting, I automatically know more than you do about being faithful in your setting. God has called you to the fun and challenge of figuring that out. Maybe this book will encourage you and facilitate your journey.

What is this book about, then? It is about a new perspective on small church life and its implications for fund-raising. I will present what I believe to be the best theological and theoretical model for understanding the small church. I will then ask and seek to answer the question, "If this is the true nature of the small church, how, then, ought we to go about meeting our financial needs?"

In Chapters 3 and 4 we will deal in significant depth with the mentality and methodology of the small church and its fund-raising efforts. In Chapters 5, 6, and 7, we will offer specific suggestions on how to respond to the three urgent crises in the small church: paying the pastor, maintaining the building, and doing Christ's mission. Chapter 8 will offer some thoughts on budgeting. In the next chapter we will offer some words of encouragement regarding the spiritual value of the financial struggle.

2

We Might Be Broke, but We Don't Need Fixin'
Economic Marginality: Problem or Solution?

"Lord, make me not so rich that I forget you; nor so poor that I curse you."
—Ancient proverb

The Problem

One of my parishioners has the irritating habit of reminding me that asking the right question is much more important than finding a quick answer. When it comes to financing the small church we ought to be pretty clear about just what the problem is. Is the problem simply financial? Is the problem as simple as "we don't have enough money"? And so, is the solution as simple as getting more money?

I serve on the National Small Church Ministry Team of the American Baptist Churches in the U.S.A. One of my colleagues there is frequently heard to query, "All right, we've been talking about this for an hour and we're not getting anywhere. So tell me, what's broke? What needs fixing?" This query frequently helps us to get a handle on how to proceed. So tell me, what's broke in the small church? Is what needs fixing in the small church the fact that we are broke? Should we proceed in the direction of fixing the financial problem?

The story is told of an incident that occurred during an every-member canvass. When the church member hesitated to commit himself, the canvasser told of his own life experience. "My wife received the report that she was pregnant. We were very happy, for we both wanted a child. I drove her to the monthly and then weekly checkups. But it galled me to pay the doctor's bills. I complained loudly as I wrote out the check. Then the baby was born—a bouncing, healthy little boy. But again I complained as I paid the hospital bill. Then we had to buy clothing, diapers, baby food, toys, and special furniture. I loved my child, but I was not at all pleased with the dent in my pocketbook that this kid was causing. Then it came time for bicycles, summer camp, baseball equipment, and ice skates. The list seemed to go on forever. But that was nothing compared to the cost of the orthodontic work he needed. For three years I nursed my resentment over that! He was growing up happy and healthy and I loved him, but he was costing me a small fortune. Then high school and extra car insurance and special summer courses. And again I complained about the cost. But those costs were trivial compared to college. Tuition and books and travel. It felt like I was going to the poorhouse. Sure, he worked every summer, but at Christian camps. And you know what they pay! And then halfway through his last semester of college he was killed in an automobile accident." Tears ran down the man's cheeks as he finished his story. "Since the funeral he hasn't cost me a penny."

Some things cost. But they are worth it. And some things money can't buy. And some things we will work night and day on, never counting the cost, so important are they to us. I don't think the basic problem in the small church is economic. I don't think the fundamental issue in the small church is financial. Certainly money is an issue (otherwise why bother writing and reading this book?). But I don't believe it is *the* issue. *The* issue often is that we *think* money is the issue. *The* issue is that we feel that economic marginality is a problem to be overcome. Could it be, rather, the method of God's operating? Could economic marginality be a component of the faithful

Christian lifestyle? Could the goads against which we have been kicking be God's attempt to make God's presence known?

Let us consider theological, biblical, and psychological perspectives on economic marginality.

A Theological Perspective

The small church is limited. But some things cannot be judged quantitatively. A Rembrandt would not be better if it were larger. A Beethoven symphony would not be better by being longer. In fact, each might well be weakened by any addition to it. Not everything is made better by being made bigger.

For example, it is absurd to try to judge the health and worth of a family by its size. We assess a family as it should be assessed: by the maturity of the individual members, the love they share together, the personal growth that they occasion for one another, by how well the next generation succeeds the first, and so on. Fortune 500 companies may want to judge their success on such criteria as percent increase of gross sales, percent of increase in profits, and so forth. Those may be appropriate measures for corporate America, but they are not appropriate measures for judging our families. Why, then, do we in the church, especially the small church, feel a need to measure our success as if we were a corporation? In fact, we are a family, the very family of God.

The health of the small church is not to be found in how rapidly it can grow until it outgrows the stigma of small budgets, small membership, and small-scale ministries. Rather, the health of the small church can be found in how joyfully and creatively and productively we have learned to live within our limits. Small churches by our very nature live face to face with our limits. We know what it means to be able to pay the fuel bill or the pastor, but not both. We know what it means to want to start another Sunday School class and to go through that well-worn and all too small list of members and not come up with one person who is both willing and able to teach. The small church is always on the edge of its limits.

The World Is Limited

But I'm not discouraged by the small church's limitations. In fact, I am quite encouraged. And that makes me out of step with society. We live in a day and age where limits are considered nothing more than obstacles to be overcome and irritations to be done away with. It is not enough to own a house, have a good job and a happy family when the Joneses have two houses, two jobs, and two sets of kids. Our place in God's scheme of things is finite and subservient, but our egos and our appetites are infinite. This is the essence of sin: that we refuse to accept the place God has given us.

The Bible is clear about our rightful place. The first stories of Genesis make this plain. For example, the Tower of Babel was built so that humankind could transcend the limited and finite roles they found themselves in, that they could ascend into the heavens and claim the prerogatives of the Infinite One. But God confounded humankind and refused to allow them to transcend their limited, finite status. Only God is infinite. Only God has no natural limits. When, in biology, tissues refuse to accept their boundaries, cancer and death result. At one time everyone believed that the earth's resources were infinite, but a quick glance at the headlines of any newspaper will point to the realization that this attitude has led to pollution and depletion, bankruptcy and revolution. The world is finite. There are objective limits and boundaries that constrain our behavior. We must learn to live with a perspective and a theology that deals with these limits. We must reject as unrealistic and as sinful philosophies of life that call for ever increasing numbers.

I am not saying that churches should not grow in members, ministry, and money. What I am saying is that numerical growth in and of itself is not a success criterion. Faithfulness, spiritual growth, and service are. And the small church, by already living on the edge of its limits, is in a natural position to embody and demonstrate those values that are spiritually healthy and life giving.

God Is Not Limited by Our Limits

This truth makes the First Baptist Church of Burnside, Iowa, full of joy and creativity. A dozen families comprise that congregation, and they are always overshadowed by the big Lutheran church just down the street. What program could they possibly do to which their Lutheran brothers and sisters couldn't bring more bodies, energy, and finances? Well, the one thing they could do was to be themselves—to enjoy living and growing and serving their Lord together and offer their very lives together as a witness. To do this, every year they choose a theme around which they will center their worship, their education, their devotional study, and their service to the community. They pick themes that are biblical, fun, and about which they can be creative. A few years ago they picked "Thankful Living" as their theme. They spent the year learning about gratitude, counting their blessings, and finding new ways to be thankful.

But that wasn't enough. They lived in a community and wanted to say thanks to their fellow townspeople. So they held a special ceremony to which they invited their whole town. Individuals, businesses, and organizations were commended for their service to the public good. Burnside had never seen anything like it. The whole town came out to affirm one another and give thanks for those good things that they shared together. Two years later people were still talking about that simple ceremony, for it had a profound impact on the whole town. You see, the town of Burnside had peaked and was slipping. The economy was weakening year by year. The young were moving out. Subtly but surely the attitude developed that there was no future in Burnside. People had become discouraged about themselves, their town, their prospects. Then those crazy Baptists, all two dozen of them, spent $13.72, or whatever it was, and in one afternoon affected the psychology of the town. To be sure, the economy didn't change for the better, but the people did. They started praising God for the half of the cup that was full instead of being depressed about the half that was empty.

Limits

Those Burnside Baptists have limits: a part-time pastor who commutes from another town; a budget so low it could double and they would still be below their denomination's minimum level; an attendance so sparse you'd barely have to take your shoes off to count them! They're limited, and they know it. But that doesn't stop them. They simply look for ways to serve and live and love within those limits, and they find them—every year, every week, every day. Because they have, they can serve as a symbol of hope for a society whose watchwords are "grow ever bigger," "waste ever more," and "never look back."

If we are ever to be a faithful and righteous society, it will be small churches like Burnside Baptist, like yours and like mine, that will be leading the way. The church has learned too much from IBM and ITT. Small churches must learn to reflect Jesus Christ—utterly limited, utterly weak, utterly lacking in resources, and yet used mightily by God to accomplish God's purposes precisely because he was limited.

"When I am weak, then am I strong," writes the apostle Paul, for in our weakness, in our limitations and constraints is the power of God made manifest. If we take the biblical witness seriously, it is through the weak, the powerless, and the limited that God chooses to act. Our limits do not in any way limit God. Rather, they serve to remind us to give God the glory!

A Biblical Perspective

Those who desire independence and self-sufficiency will be disillusioned by the Word of God. Those who would organize God's mission without depending on God are in for a surprise. One thing the Bible is very clear about: It is we who are dependent on God, not God on us. God is not dependent upon human resources to accomplish divine purposes. God uses human resources but in such a way as to underscore God's freedom, sovereignty, and creativity. God does not need our wealth—personal or financial—to achieve God's intentions. Instead, God uses faith and obedience.

Consider Abraham, undoubtedly a wealthy merchant of Ur. He could have done lots for God by being faithful and generous at home. But God called him to leave his economic base, to go to an unknown land, to believe in unbelievable promises. And he did it. And . . . well, you know the rest of the story.

Or Sarah. She was well beyond the years of childbearing when God promised her a son. Though she thought the proposition laughable, in due time she bore the promised son.

Or Moses. A tongue-tied fugitive. But calling him, God equipped him to set his people free.

Or Joshua. Who ever heard of destroying a walled and fortified city with the blasts of trumpets and the shouts of soldiers? What, no high-cost battering rams, no highly paid long distance archers or expensive protracted siege? Joshua didn't need them with God on his side.

Or Deborah. By God's command, she called on ill-equipped, outnumbered, undisciplined, ragtag mountain warriors of Israel to battle the iron chariots of Jabin. So poor the odds, so preposterous the call that Barak would only consent to it if Deborah went along, presumably reasoning that she wouldn't risk her own life! But she did and he did and Israel did. And God's people won an incredible victory.

Or David. Outraged that an overgrown pagan should insult the army of the living God, he marched into conflict shorn of every weapon save five stones and one sling. God used him to win a victory totally out of proportion to the ability and resources of the Israelites.

And, if space permitted, we could go on and on with the stories of God's victories— victories unpredictable on the basis of the material at hand! We learn very clearly from the stories of the Old Testament that God is not constrained by limitations on available resources. In fact, poverty of material resources often turns attention all the more clearly to the God who is working out divine purposes in the course of human history. Thus material poverty becomes a goad to spiritual sufficiency. Zechariah summarized the accomplishments recorded in the Old Testament with these words: "Not by might, nor by power, but by my Spirit, says the LORD" (Zechariah 4:6).

In the New Testament too, this theme is given clear articulation. Jesus taught his disciples to pray for their daily bread, to avoid storing up earthly treasures (knowing how easily our hearts are seduced), not to worry about food, drink, clothing, or the morrow, for God knows our needs. Rather, Jesus instructs us to seek first God's kingdom and God's righteousness and not concentrate on secondary things; they will fall into place. And Jesus practiced what he preached—feeding thousands from five loaves and two fishes, paying the tax with the coin in the fish's mouth (see Matthew 17:27), "borrowing" an ass's colt to ride into Jerusalem, to name but a few instances.

Jesus' message is not only that we don't need an economic surfeit to do God's work but also that a financial abundance gets in the way of accomplishing God's purpose.

The rich young ruler went away sad *because he had much goods*. ". . . It is easier for a camel to go through the eye of a needle than for a rich man to enter the kingdom of God," Jesus said (Matthew 19:24). And he told the story of the man whose "invested funds" were so great that he decided to build even bigger barns. So preoccupied was this man with the wrong things that his soul was required of him. Instead of securing a comfortable life, he achieved his own demise. This is the paradox of Christ's teaching. The person who seeks to gain his or her life shall lose it. Only the one who loses his or her life for Christ's sake gains it. (Haven't you seen churches shrivel up and die because they tried to insure their survival through endowment funds? And how often have you seen true life in a small church joyfully struggling to be faithful to Christ's calling?)

The early church in Jerusalem did not hesitate to live on the edge, trusting God to supply. They did two things churches today would consider anathema: pooling resources and spending broke. This did not insure their long-term survival, but it did assure their integrity during their existence. I wonder if churches today would be healthier if more were asking the integrity question instead of the existence question.

And throughout the remainder of the New Testament, the church was continually being cautioned about the dangers of riches, the subtle shift from trusting in God's power to trusting in one's own resources. Paul reminded the Corinthians:

Take yourselves . . . at the time when you were called: how many of you were wise in the ordinary sense of the word, how many were influential people, or came from noble families? No, it was to shame the wise that God chose what is foolish by human reckoning, and to shame what is strong that he chose what is weak by human reckoning; those whom the world thinks common and contemptible are the ones that God has chosen—those who are nothing at all to show up those who are everything (1 Corinthians 1:26-29, *Jerusalem Bible*).

. . .

For God's foolishness is wiser than human wisdom, and God's weakness is stronger than human strength. . . . As scripture says: *If anyone wants to boast, let him boast about the Lord* (1 Corinthians 1:25, 31, *Jerusalem Bible*).

James reminded the congregations under his care:

My brothers, do not try to combine faith in Jesus Christ, our glorified Lord, with the making of distinctions between classes of people. Now suppose a man comes into your synagogue, beautifully dressed and with a gold ring on, and at the same time a poor man comes in, in shabby clothes, and you take notice of the well-dressed man, and say, "Come this way to the best seats"; then you tell the poor man, "Stand over there" or "You can sit on the floor by my footrest." Can't you see that you have used two different standards in your mind, and turned yourselves into judges, and corrupt judges at that?

Listen, my dear brothers: it was those who are poor according to the world that God chose, to be rich in faith and to be the heirs to the kingdom which he promised to those who love him. In spite of this, you have no respect for anybody who is poor (James 2:1-7, *Jerusalem Bible*).

. . .

Now an answer for the rich. Start crying, weep for the miseries that are coming to you. Your wealth is all rotting, your clothes are all eaten up by moths. All your gold and your silver are corroding away, and the same corrosion will be your own sentence, and eat into your body. It was a burning fire that you stored up as your treasure for the last days. . . . On earth you have had a life of comfort and luxury; in the time of slaughter you went on eating to your heart's content (James 5:1-3, 5, *Jerusalem Bible*).

And John in his vision cautioned the church in Laodicea:

"'You say to yourself, "I am rich, I have made a fortune, and have everything I want," never realizing that you are wretchedly and pitiably poor, and blind and naked too. I warn you, buy from me the gold that has been tested in the fire to make you really rich, and white robes to clothe you and cover your shameful nakedness, and eye ointment to put on your eyes so that you are able to see, I *am* the one *who reproves and disciplines all those he loves:* so repent in real earnest'" (Revelation 3:17-19, *Jerusalem Bible*).

One thing is very clear in Scripture, God's purposes are accomplished, not with abundant resources, not ever in spite of the lack of resources, but because of our poverty!

A Psychological Perspective

I had a dream the other night in which I was approached by a salesman in a three-piece suit. He opened his briefcase and handed me his "product." It was a book, well bound and nicely printed, with my name in gilt letters on the cover. Since I had always desired to be an author, I was pleased, until I realized that it was not a book by me. Rather, it was a book about me. My breathing quickened. It was, he was saying, the story of my life, complete and unabridged. I opened to the table of contents: "The Joy of Childhood," "The Pain of Adolescence," "The Curiosity of College." The dates and subtitles were all true to my life story. Complete, did he say? I looked further. The dates went right on through the present into the future! I slammed the book shut, my heart pounding. "It is all there," he said, smiling at me. "Don't you want to know how it is all going to come out? How your children will do in life? Whether Judson will publish your manuscript? Whether your parish will wax or wane? Whether your life will actually amount to anything? Go ahead and read it," he said. "You don't have to pay me now. You can pay me later." And he began to chuckle.

His chuckling turned into laughter, and his laughter into hysterics, and his eyes blazed. I woke up kicking and screaming and bathed in a cold sweat.

I was tempted. I'll admit it. Part of me really wanted to see how it was all going to come out. Whether it would be worth all the blood, sweat, and tears. But that part of me is the temptable and contemptible part of me. The real me, the strong me, the faithful me doesn't want to be robbed of life. The Christ in me believes that how it is going to end depends on how I act and react and interact with whatever life sends my way at any moment. The Christ in me believes that the blood, sweat, and tears *is* life. That the quest is life. That to be alive is an adventure. That to wrestle all night with challenges, like Jacob, is to know God. The kingdom of God is always one step beyond us. To struggle to take that step, despite the discouragement of others, the pooh-poohing of society, to keep on struggling to take that step—that is the stuff of life. ". . . Keep faithful, and I will give you the crown of life . . ." says Jesus (Revelation 2:10, *Jerusalem Bible*).

Our outcomes are not fixed before we struggle. The score of our lives is not determined before the game is played. The fate of our parish is not simply a deduction from GNP and demographic data. Rather, how we play will go a long way in determining the outcome. This is the adventure of life. Faith is a grand quest. Our faith calls us to believe the unbelievable, work for the impossible, envision the unimaginable. Our faith calls us to root for the underdog, whether it be David against Goliath, Jesus against the Jerusalem authorities, or our parish against our budget. In fact, our faith calls us to *be* the underdog, to venture forth in campaigns that are against the odds. Paul wrote to the Corinthians that God brings into being that which does not yet exist. Isn't this part of the great adventure of our faith, to make real by our God-graced efforts a part of his kingdom which by earthly standards cannot be? This is what captures the spirit of men and women—the excitement of adventure, the challenge of risk for a great and eternal good.

"Fat" churches may never know the thrill of adventure. The

joy of trusting *in God* to supply what is necessary to accomplish God's will is unknown by those congregations that only budget dollars that are already in sight. But there is a positive psychology possible in economic marginality. It is exciting to know the future depends on you. It is thrilling to see your efforts blessed by God and your hopes, step by step, becoming reality. It is joy to step out in faith and see God build foundations under your castles. To wrestle with a challenge and keep on wrestling with it until it yields its blessing is to experience life. Now not all blessings are to be found in success stories, narrowly defined in financial terms. Sometimes, like ancient Israel, we see our place of worship abandoned, and we seem to survive only in spiritual exile. But, remember, it was in exile that the Torah was shaped, the synagogue formed, and the prophecies of the Messiah given. Exile is but a prolonged adventure. Jesus calls us to abundant life. This we experience not in a faith statement, but in a faith adventure. The small, struggling church is in the position to live this adventure to the full.

Listen to the *joy* of a small church that took a great leap of faith and landed on its feet. (Helen Louise is a staff member of the American Baptist Churches of Rhode Island.)

Dear Helen Louise,

Here is my belated report on the progress of our every-member canvass. As I may have told you, the Georgiaville Baptist Church had not had a membership canvass in years. It seems that some people had been offended by previous attempts and tactics. So I suggested to them that we sit down with the boards and work out a reasonable budget for the year, something which had not been done in years as well. They had existed on a hand-to-mouth basis.

After the budget was arrived at, we proposed a plan to initiate interest in the church giving. First, a letter was sent out to all the members and friends of the church, in which we coveted their support so that the church could more effectively serve the people and the community.

A series of three sermons was prepared based on the theme "Free to Love, Free to Live, and Free to Give." The emphasis in all the sermons was the need for effective stewardship in our church. Two weeks before Loyalty Sunday, a letter was sent out enclosing the proposed budget. A pledge card was also enclosed, and everyone was asked to bring his or her card on Loyalty Sunday. If some were unable to attend worship that day, they were encouraged to mail in the cards. Realizing that the previous year only 18 pledges had been received, we were delighted to receive 32 pledges the first Sunday. We followed up the remaining pledges with telephone calls and a second letter asking those who had not done so to send or bring their pledges in by the following week. The second week our pledges increased by ten, making our total 42.

A further follow-up by letter increased our pledges to the present 48. With a membership of 74, and realizing that many of these pledges are husband and wife and family pledges, we noted that over 80 percent of our members had pledged. When the final amounts were tallied, we had oversubscribed our budget by over $700!

Our church family is delighted with what they have done—so much so that they wrote [the state denominational office] stating that they would not need the $900 supplement which they had been receiving. In addition we have exceeded all our special offerings goals, for which we are most grateful.

Praying, preaching, and publicity have done the job for us. In addition, a new awareness of the sense of stewardship is apparent in our church family, and we thank God for it.

Cordially,
Camille Bedard[1]

Conclusion

The church that lives on the edge lives in the position of faithfulness. Its life is a struggle, and its victories are from God. But the position of faithfulness has an end towards which it is aimed. The life of the small church has an *integrity* which it seeks to embody fully. It is to this aspect of our explorations that we now turn our attention—the integrity of the small church. What is its nature?

3

Ralph's Kind of Church

The Obvious Secret Nature of the Small Church

Let's Take a Quick Trip to Garrison Keillor's Lake Wobegon

What's so special about this town is not the food, though Ralph's Pretty Good Grocery has got in a case of fresh cod. Frozen, but it's fresher than what's been in his freezer for months. In the grocery business, you have to throw out stuff sometimes, but Ralph is Norwegian and it goes against his principles. People bend down and peer into the meat case. "Give me a pork loin," they say. "One of those in the back, one of the pink ones." "These in front are better," he says. "They're more aged. You get better flavor." But they want a pink one, so Ralph takes out a pink one, bites his tongue. This is the problem with being in retail, you can't say what you think.

More and more people are sneaking off to the Higgledy-Piggledy in St. Cloud, where you find two acres of food, a meat counter a block long with huge walloping roasts and steaks big enough to choke a cow, and exotic fish lying on crushed ice. Once Ralph went to his brother Benny's for dinner and Martha put baked swordfish on the table. Ralph's face burned. His own sister-in-law! "It's delicious," said Mrs. Ralph. "Yeah," Ralph said, "if it wasn't for the mercury poisoning, I'd take swordfish every day of the week." Cod, he pointed out, is farther down in the food chain, and doesn't collect the mercury that the big fish do. Forks paused in midair. He would have gone on to describe the effects of mercury on the body, how it lodges in the brain, wiping the slate clean until you wind up in bed attached to tubes and can't remember your own Zip Code, but his wife contacted him on his ankle. Later, she said, "You had no business saying that."

"I'll have no business, period," he said, "if people don't wake up."

"Well, it's a free country, and she has a perfect right to go shop where she wants to."

"Sure she does, and she can go live there, too."

When the Thanatopsis Club hit its centennial in 1982 and Mrs. Hallberg wrote to the White House and asked for an essay from the President on small-town life, she got one, two paragraphs that extolled Lake Wobegon as a model of free enterprise and individualism, which was displayed in the library under glass, although the truth is that Lake Wobegon survives to the extent that it does on a form of voluntary socialism with elements of Deism, fatalism, and nepotism. Free enterprise runs on self-interest. This is socialism, and it runs on loyalty. You need a toaster, you buy it at Co-op Hardware even though you can get a deluxe model with all the toaster attachments for less money at K-Mart in St. Cloud. You buy it at Co-op because you know Otto. Glasses you will find at Clifford's which also sells shoes and ties and some gloves. (It is trying to be the department store it used to be when it was The Mercantile, which it is still called by most people because the old sign is so clear on the brick facade, clearer than the "Clifford's" in the window.) Though you might rather shop for glasses in a strange place where they'll encourage your vanity, though Clifford's selection of frames is clearly based on Scripture ("Take no thought for what you shall wear. . . .") and you might put a hideous piece of junk on your face and Clifford would say, "I think you'll like those" as if you're a person who looks like you don't care what you look like—nevertheless you should think twice before you get the Calvin Klein glasses from Vanity Vision in the St. Cloud Mall. Calvin Klein isn't going to come with the Rescue Squad and he isn't going to teach your children about redemption by grace. You couldn't find Calvin Klein to save your life.

If people were to live by comparison shopping, the town would go bust. It cannot compete with other places item by item. Nothing in town is quite as good as it appears to be somewhere else. If you live there, you have to take it as a whole. That's loyalty. This is why Judy Ingqvist does not sing "Holy City" on Sunday morning, although everyone says she sounds great on "Holy City"—it's not her wish to sound great, though she is the leading soprano; it's her wish that all the sopranos sound at least okay. So she sings quietly. One Sunday when the Ingqvists went to the Black Hills on vacation, a young, white-knuckled seminarian filled in; he gave a forty-five minute sermon and had a lot of sermon left over when finally three deacons cleared their throats simultaneously. They sounded like German shepherds barking, and their barks meant that the congregation now knew that he was bright and he had nothing more to prove to them. The young man looked on the sermon as free enterprise. You work like hell on it and come up with a winner. He wanted to give it all the best that was in him, of which he had more than he needed. He was opening a Higgledy-Piggledy of theology, and the barks were meant to remind him where he was in Lake Wobegon, where smart doesn't count for so much. A minister has to be able to read a clock. At noon, it's time to go home and turn up the pot roast and get the peas out of the freezer. Everybody gets their pot roast at Ralph's. It's not the tenderest meat in the Ninth Federal Reserve District, but after you bake it for four hours until it falls apart in shreds, what's the difference? [1]

From Ralph to You

Your small church may be a "fer piece" from Lake Wobegon. To go there in a book on small church stewardship may seem like quite a detour. But the fact of the matter is that unless we go through Ralph's mind, we will never get to the small church! Stewardship in the small church is different in theology and in practice from other settings. Successful fund-raising in the small church must be done in harmony with the small church's unique nature. Constructive stewardship activity in the small church starts with solid understandings of the small church. A consideration of Ralph's Pretty Good Grocery and the St. Cloud Higgledy-Piggledy is a helpful starting place to gain this understanding. So let us look into each of these worlds a little more deeply. Let us use our imaginations to fill in the details of the lives of Ralph and the Higgledy-Piggledy store manager. The kinds of things we would imagine about their lives might fall into four general categories: context, organization, social, and society.

What does the world look like and feel like to the manager of the Higgledy-Piggledy? First of all there is a particular **context** to the world in which he lives and moves and has his being. In all likelihood he grew up in a suburb with easy access to the urban center with all its stores, events, educational opportunities, and a daily newspaper to tell all about it. Therefore, he is used to a relatively large population center like St. Cloud, although St. Cloud is far from the home of his youth. Along with the large number of people in his world is the reality that he currently knows only a small fraction of them. And this fraction is getting smaller because each year 20 to 25 percent of his friends will move and be replaced by strangers. Of course, he hopes to move on soon, too. If he does a good job in St. Cloud, maybe a store in Minneapolis will open up for him.

The truth is that the economic **organization** to which he belongs is the center of his world. His employer is, by and large, very fair. Upper-level management has set growth goals for the company, and our store manager is very clear about how he fits into them. Although he has not been above doing a little politicking from time to time, he is quite confident that things will go as they ought to go. To the degree that he manages efficiently, reaches the quotas set for him (through a very rational, logical, and objective procedure), plays by the rules, and above all, stays well in the black, he will be rewarded. To the degree he fails to do those things, his years of hard work with the company won't count for much. Though he and the regional manager get on well, he would expect to be fired if he didn't perform. This arrangement seems quite fair to him, especially since he has no intention of failing.

His **social** world consists of a few friends and his work associates. Although he has a competent group of people working with him and there is little interpersonal strife at work, he would hesitate to call them friends. He feels he treats them

well, paying them the going wage for the functions they perform. Since he could never get to know all the baggers and
check-out people personally (because of their numbers and
high rate of turnover), he has despaired of relating personally
to all but a few trusted lieutenants. Of these he prefers the
younger ones because they are less set in their ways and aren't
fixated on what worked yesterday. The most ambitious of
these, he knows, only pretend to be team players, waiting for
their moment of personal opportunity. In the meantime he is
confident that he can continue to manage the exchange of ener-
gies and loyalties with them to his advantage.

This relationship between boss and bossed would be stifling
and frustrating if not for the fluidity of contemporary society.
Our manager knows that St. Cloud is but a stepping-stone.
The particular lessons he learns here he can carry with him to
any of a thousand other communities as he works his way
upward, for on the variables that matter to him, all these communities are the same. Though he didn't finish college, he
knows that he has been highly trained for his job. He is very
aggressive about continuing training programs. He is hardly
aware of it, but he is driven by the twin fears of being under-
trained in a world of specialists and being overspecialized in an
economy that is rapidly changing in structure. Personally he is
very happy at home. His second wife understands him much
better than his first, and the three sets of kids have finally come
to accept each other.

What a shock it would be for our Higgledy-Piggledy manager to wake up one morning to find that he was the owner of
Ralph's Pretty Good Grocery! Ralph lives in a totally different
world. But since Ralph grew up here and has experienced little
else, he finds his world to be a congenial one—happy and very
different. The context of Ralph's world can be summed up with
the words "old" and "stable." Ralph is actually Ralph Junior.
His father founded the store. So as far back as anyone can
remember, there has been a Ralph at Ralph's Pretty Good Grocery. And the store is pretty much what it has always been.
Ralph made some inventory and display changes when he took

over the store, despite the predictions of bankruptcy from Ralph Senior. Apparently these innovations used up all his creative juices because there haven't been any major changes since. Ralph does keep up with the latest Maxwell House products, but he hesitates to do anything really radical. "So few like tofu," he has been heard to remark. One summer a university marketing student surveyed and questionnaired to his heart's content and found that Ralph actually could turn a modest profit on tofu if he stocked it in three flavors and displayed it in the front window. Ralph told him where he could put the tofu. Ralph Senior once sold tofu, but that was during the war when you sold whatever you could get. Well, not exactly sold. You kind of put it on layaway. You gave the customers the goods and laid away the bill until they could pay. It still warms Ralph Senior's heart to know how many families he helped to keep body and soul together during those times. And also it warms his heart to remember that every cent owed him was paid up eventually. Maybe living shoulder to shoulder with people keeps them honest. Or maybe they got tired of being beholden. But, whatever, they paid. When they signed the bill in lieu of cash, Ralph Senior would always ease the tension by chuckling, "Don't worry. I know where you live!" Which, of course, he did.

Ralph's world is made up of a smaller number of people, a virtually unvarying cast of characters who live in connection with the soil and with one another. What keeps them together is not that one needs groceries and the other sells them, but the sheer fact that they are in it together. The glue in Ralph's world is not people's functions, but their place in the common social fabric. They do what they do so that they can be.

One good thing about Ralph's **organization** is that you can walk in off the street and talk to the boss. In fact, so many people do just that, that it seems kind of funny to use the terms "organization" and "Ralph's Pretty Good" in the same breath. Ralph really isn't organized, at least not in a way that our Higgledy-Piggledy manager would recognize. Oh sure, Ralph orders groceries, stocks them, collects the money, and pays the bills. But still he is not *organized*. Nothing is written down except in Ralph's head. This didn't help much when he went to the Small Business Administration about a loan. Needless to say, he didn't get it. But Ralph figures, considering all the bother with paperwork he has saved over the years and how much of his brain he is using that would otherwise lie fallow, that he is a little bit to the good.

And of course it helps to have nothing written down, including the prices, because when poor widow Fox comes in, he can charge her half price without nicking her pride. This impulse to generosity on his part almost caused a problem one day when all three poor widows in town did their shopping at the same hour. It dawned on Ralph, after the last had left, that if this kept up, he would slowly but surely end up in the hole. But what to do? Ralph sat himself down to think this one over. He felt that maybe for the first time in twenty years a policy decision was in the works. After all, he had the future to think about. That subject was not an easy one for Ralph to consider (therefore the seated position). His wife's "What do you think you're doing when we've got all these cases to unpack?" just showed she did not understand the gravity of the occasion or the difficulty of the enterprise. Somewhere in the midst of all this thinking Ralph asked the Lord for some wisdom. No sooner had he re-opened his eyes than who should swagger into the store but that rich city fellow who just bought the old Pullen place. Immediately that week's Sunday School verse popped into Ralph's head: "He has filled the hungry with good things, and the rich he has sent empty away" (Luke 1:53). Ralph figured the "empty" ought to apply to the man's wallet. So when the man with the irritating swagger came to check out, Ralph just added back in the loss from the widow ladies. Just like Naomi and Boaz, he reasoned. Even when Ralph thought forward, he thought backwards.

Unlike the Higgledy-Piggledy manager, Ralph lives in a very small **society**. It is not United States society or even Minnesotan society, although that is closer. It is a society of the people he knows and knows of. It is here, as it has always been.

Nobody is too highfalutin to do what he or she has to do to get by and stay put. If the people specialize in anything, it is in a whole and full life. Ralph's **social** world is just about equal to his society. The people here are valued for who they are and because they are connected to one another. Since each generation does more or less the same things at the same time, the older one is the wiser. And here, "sticking it out," not being smart, is what counts for much. Ralph and his wife have friends. They are close, but not too intimate. When you live that close, you need a bit of space.

The Higgledy-Piggledy world and Ralph's Pretty Good world are nearly opposite poles on the spectrum of the ways in which human beings organize their lives together. Much can be said about this spectral understanding of human societies: (1) it can be said that this formulation is nothing new (although it seems to be pretty much forgotten today); (2) the dynamics that occur when these two types of societies meet can be described; and (3) the potency of this understanding of human organization for effective small church ministry can be demonstrated.

Nothing New

That the poles of human life look remarkably like the Higgledy-Piggledy-Ralph's spectrum can be traced in modern thought at least as far back as Ferdinand Tonnies's seminal work, *Community and Society*, published in 1887.[2] He proposed a polarity in human society which he labeled Gesellschaft and Gemeinschaft. Gesellschaft is a form of social organization in which "social relationships are formal, contractual, expedient, impersonal and specialized. . . . Gesellschaft is most typically approximated in modern urban society . . . because of its weak family organization, the emphasis on utilitarian goods, and the impersonal and competitive nature and of its social relationships."[3] Gemeinschaft is the opposite type of social organization in which "social bonds are based on close personal ties of friendship and kinship. . . . [It is] characterized by the predominance of intimate primary relationships and by emphasis upon tradition, consensus, informality and kinship."[4]

Robert Redfield[5] published an article in 1947 in which he postulated a "Folk Society" and an "Urban Society" at the opposite ends of a spectrum of social forms. This spectrum became clear to him when he compared his own background to that of the "native" Central American tribes with whom he was doing anthropological fieldwork. His article delineated certain essential characteristics of the folk society, and it sparked much interest in the comparative understanding of societies by placing them on a folk-urban continuum.

I do not conceive of Tonnies's and Redfield's work as "new." Rather, I see them as giving sociological and anthropological articulation to a great social reality that runs throughout the biblical account. In Genesis 12 God promised to make of Abram a great **people.** In Deuteronomy 7 the calling and love of God is expressed toward this smallest group of people. The unfolding story of God's relationship with God's "people" occupies the rest of the Old Testament. The mission of the Christ was to make foreigners and aliens fellow citizens with *God's people* (Ephesians 2:19). And the eternal reality of those who follow Christ is described by Peter: "You are a chosen *people,* a royal priesthood, a holy nation, a *people* belonging to God, that you may declare the praises of him who called you out of darkness into his wonderful light. Once you were not a *people,* but now you are the *people of God . . .*" (1 Peter 2:9-10, NIV, italics added). We are used to thinking of the biblical term "people" in a theological sense. There is nothing wrong with that, but since the theological meaning intended by the authors assumes a common sociological understanding of the term "people," we might do well to remember what the biblical word means sociologically.

> People in general do not exist; there are only particular peoples. Each people has a separate and cohesive actuality of its own. Every person belongs to a particular tongue or nation or tribe; and this people is not reducible to the mathematical aggregate of its members. The people defines the person; its existence is

determinative of who he is. Humanity is not visualized as a world-wide census of individuals, but as the separate peoples that, taken together, comprise mankind as a whole. Each people retains its own discrete unity. Therefore, to identify a particular society as the people of God is immediately to set it over against all other peoples. This people and it alone has been constituted in a special way by this God's action, by his taking it "for his own possession." Henceforth, it can be spoken of as his people. . . . In some respects this people is like other peoples. Yet in other respects, and in respects that are intrinsic to its character, it is unlike any other people.[6]

So the biblical term "people" means something very nearly akin to Gemeinschaft of Tonnies and the folk society of Redfield. Ralph's world is not heaven on earth. But in the life together of God's people, Ralph would recognize the fulfillment of all he held to be near and dear and right. The Higgledy-Piggledy manager, on the other hand, will be quite surprised by heaven.

When Societies Meet

Thus we see that Ralph's world is nothing new. It is the venerable way that humans have organized themselves. It is even the human experience appealed to by the biblical authors when they wanted to point us to the qualities of eternity. It is venerable but it is also vulnerable, for in virtually every confrontation with the forces of modernity,[7] it suffers loss. Ralph was realistic to worry about the Higgledy-Piggledy store swallowing up his business. The sad saga of the Native Americans graphically demonstrates just how poorly a tribal society fares in a Gesellschaft world.

And we small church pastors who desire to and do live in the Lake Wobegons of this world and have plenty of Ralphs in our congregation have an all-pervasive feeling of powerlessness and hopelessness. Intuitively we recoil when a Higgledy-Piggledy denominational official gives us his tools to renew and rebuild and refinance our church. Like David struggling to don Saul's armor, we know it doesn't fit us. And we know that even if it did, it would just turn us into one more Higgledy-

Piggledy. When Ralph's world collides with the world of Higgledy-Piggledy, the outcome is inevitably on the side of Higgledy-Piggledy. And yet . . . Ralph's world never does quite disappear, does it? Just when it looked as though the forces of Higgledy-Piggledy had won, people started moving out of the suburbs. Not back to Eden of course, but back to where they could garden . . . and get back in touch with the soil . . . and with people . . . and sink down roots . . . and live in harmony with God, nature, and their fellow men and women. This exurban life is a compromise, of course, but it reveals that there is some need, some drive, some restlessness in our soul that won't be happy until it finds its own version of Ralph's world. That is what the Higgledy-Piggledy manager really wants, but he doesn't know it. That is why, though individual small churches go bankrupt and die, the small church never does. For there is something fundamentally human (and divine) to be found there.

The Small Church Implication

So we come now to the connection between Ralph's world and effective ministry in the small church. It is imperative if we are to give quality leadership in the small church that we realize that there is more than one way in which human groups organize themselves. Most of us have been trained to think and live and have been given tools and ways of doing things from the other way of living. We need, therefore, to relearn the ways of the small church. Those who are effective small church leaders operate on this understanding intuitively even if without cognitive tools. But many experience frustration and weakness in ministry because they are attempting to minister with Higgledy-Piggledy tools in Ralph's world. If we are to relearn the ways of the small church, we could do no better than to look anew at Robert Redfield's understanding of the folk society. When I first discovered his 1947 article in the *American Journal of Sociology*, it was as if a light bulb went on in my head. My "Eurekas," "Ahas," and excited pacing and gesturing convinced my wife of what she feared about me all along! However, I soon came back down to earth equipped with a whole new understanding of how to live and lead in the small church. Redfield's article is too long to reproduce in its entirety, but John A. Hostetler gives an insightful summary in his book *Amish Society,* in which he applies the folk society model to Amish society.

> The "folk" society, as conceptualized by Robert Redfield, is a small, isolated, traditional, simple, homogeneous society where oral communication and conventionalized ways are important in integrating the whole of life. In such an ideal-type society, shared practical knowledge is more important than science, custom is valued more than critical knowledge, and associations are personal and emotional rather than abstract and categoric. The idea of change is uncomfortable in a folk society. Young people do what the old people did when they were young. Members communicate intimately with each other, not only by word of mouth, but also by custom and symbols that reflect a strong sense of belonging to each other. . . . Leadership is personal rather than institutionalized. There are no gross economic inequalities. Mutual aid is characteristic of its members. The goals of life are never stated as matters of doctrine, nor are they questioned. They are implied by the acts which make up living in a small society. Custom tends to become sacred. Behavior is strongly patterned, and acts as well as cultural objects are given symbolic meaning, often pervasively religious. Religion is diffuse and all-pervasive. Planting and harvesting is as sacred in its own way as singing and praying in the typical folk society. Any given folk society may not have all of these characteristics. But by taking into account many folk societies all over the world, anthropologists have constructed a model with which to think about types of societies.[8]

At first glance it may seem absurd to lump, for example, Ralph's Lake Wobegon, Redfield's Guatemalan natives, the Amish, Native Americans, village life in medieval Europe, Australian aborigines, and the ancient tribes of Israel together as exhibiting one type of social structure. They are very different in language, dress, customs, technology, geography, and so forth. Granted there are many differences. But Redfield's genius was to see the similarities, and the similarities are found in the dynamics of their social life. I think most of us would agree with the whole generation of anthropologists since Redfield that there is indeed a real similarity of social dynamics among the many types of cultures, such as listed above. But what does that have to do with the small church?

It may seem a long jump from the folk society to the small church. And that was exactly what was worrying me as I journeyed from the friendly confines of Block Island to the great state of Ohio. The Ohio State Council of Churches had invited me to lead one-day workshops in three different parts of the state. The subject was activating small churches for mission and outreach. I was prepared to share what I felt were some exciting strategies for doing mission in the small church, but first I wanted to present the basis of these strategies. I also felt that if a clear and rich model of the small church could be communicated, each person could come up with his or her own way of proceeding to greater faithfulness. But I was anxious about this part of my presentation. I thought I was on to something, but if nobody knew what I was talking about, it was going to be three long and embarrassing days!

I presented twenty characteristics that I felt were true to small church life. After I described briefly each characteristic, I invited response and reaction. As soon as people caught on to my desire for honest feedback, we were off on a lively interaction. To my illustrations were added their experiences. Even when individuals felt that a particular characteristic didn't apply to their church, they knew plenty of small churches to which it did apply. When I finished the lists, I asked them, "Have I been talking about your church?" The overwhelming response was *yes!* And it was the same the second and third days, also. Scores and scores of people representing dozens of churches in another part of the country told me that I was accurately describing life in their parish. (These twenty characteristics put in the form of a questionnaire with which to rank your church may be found at the end of the chapter.)

Where did I get these twenty characteristics which were felt to be so indicative of small church life? I did not get them from

any analysis of the church. I did not get them from any
"Understanding Your Church" manual. I did not get them from
any theologian. I got them point for point from Redfield's folk
society article. I had seen in his description of what makes a
primitive society tick the very same dynamics that made my
own small church tick. It may seem funny to say it, but I, as a
small church pastor, felt more understood by Redfield than by
most of the people writing about renewal in the church today!
And if Redfield knew what made us tick, maybe by looking at
things from this perspective we could determine the methods
of moving to greater faithfulness in our small churches today.

Let us summarize some of the qualities of small church life
from this folk society perspective. The "small" church thus
understood is more than a numeric category. It is a type of
social organization. Among its distinguished features are a
unitary social structure, a connectedness based on personal
relationships, and a traditional basis of operating. If we take
this perspective, we can, along with Carl Dudley, define a
small church as a "single cell of caring people."[9] A small church
is a congregation in which everyone knows or expects to know
everyone else. The peopled world of each member includes the
entire membership, relatively, if not directly. Furthermore, it is
a social organism with "generations of memory." The stories of
individual members and their common faith-life are a major
part of the living reality of this social organism in the present.
The patterns of social interaction may vary from church to
church, but within each they are abundantly clear. Roles, positions, authorities, powers, and symbolic status are clearly
allocated within such a social grouping. The small church
more nearly resembles a tribe with its primary relationships
than a business corporation with its rationalized organiza-
tional charts.

We have argued that the Higgledy-Piggledy–Gesellschaft–
business world is a significantly different social universe than
the Ralph's Pretty Good–Gemeinschaft–folk society. These
differences are revealed at all levels of functioning.

Planning

Let us consider the planning process in the local church. A Higgledy-Piggledy planner would assume that planning is rational. Planning utilizes the cognitive capacities of the leadership of a local church. It assumes that the life of a corporate body can be governed by explicit, abstract, logical formulations. It assumes that the environment can be correctly apprehended through data analysis. It assumes that the primary response to need is programmatic. It looks at the present in order to determine the future. It sees the church as God's instrument in the world. None of these are wrong necessarily. But they are inappropriate to churches with different operating assumptions—those that operate on a folk society basis. If this nature of small churches were taken more into account, what characteristics would the planning tool so devised need to have in order to be more appropriate? First of all, it would take a different time perspective. It would consider the history and heritage, the past of the church, in order to come to an understanding of its present. Only then would it ask about the future. Second, it would take a different perspective on church life. People and their connections would be seen as the primary "stuff" of the church. Programming would be seen as necessary but secondary. Third, it would understand that the environment is apprehended through the filters of subjectivity, personality, and immediacy. Data, impersonal needs, or removed needs would not be held up first. And fourth, the church would not be assumed to be primarily God's *instrument* in the world, but God's *presence* in the world. This would shift the focus from programs done in order to fulfill God's will (although it would not eliminate this concern) to who we ought to be in order to fulfill God's destiny for us in this time and place.

Problem Solving

Again consider how problem solving differs between the business/science world and the tribal group. A rational approach to problem solving looks like this:

1. The problem area is frozen, and one specific problem is focused upon.
2. This problem is clearly defined (quantitatively, if possible).
3. The problem, its causes, implications, and ramifications are analyzed. What forces have brought the problem into being, keep it in place, and resist actual or potential solution efforts?
4. List solution states. Solutions must be specific, objective, recognizable, and measurable.
5. Choose solution state to be achieved (with criteria used for selection).
6. Devise an action plan with goals, objectives, and strategies, including performance and time criteria.
7. Implement action plan.
8. The problem is solved after solution is effected, generalized, and stabilized.

While Ralph's approach to problem solving might look like this:

1. The problem is noticed. This is usually an intuitive and general awareness.
2. The problem is put on "the back burner." Here it simmers for a while until an intuitive solution surfaces (or it is judged to be unsolvable!).
3. Eureka! A solution that fits who we are as much as it fits the problem is discerned.
4. Good news. This discovery is shared with the rest of the folk, frequently in a form attributing divine origin.
5. Vocation. Called to this response, it will be held as a matter of faith.

Or consider how different outreach looks when viewed by a large church as opposed to a small church.

Mission

Mission at the Higgledy-Piggledy manager's church is understood to be something the church does in the form of a program. The need for a mission program would be registered by objective criteria, frequently statistical. The success of the ministry could be demonstrated in quantifiable terms. The mission program would be promoted within the church by disseminating information about a problem "out there." The program would be developed logically. Its promoters would be sure they could successfully defend it at the board meeting, and it would be implemented through the ability of the church to organize the resources available to it.

Mission at Ralph's church is quite different. It is something the church members are—loving, concerned, friendly, caring. It is done by persons with persons on the face-to-face level. How successful this mission is is assessed subjectively, as is the need to which it responds in the first place! The enhancement of this type of outreach effort hinges on its being perceived as close to home, connected to self, and preserving or furthering the well-being of the whole. The response is intuitive and predicated upon God's ability to work miracles!

Pickup Trucks and Pledge Cards

The small church social system has its own unique essence. Knowing it and loving it is the only basis upon which we can build. But this is a book about fund-raising. What does the folk society model have to teach us in the small church about that? What motivates giving in such a social system?

Well, let's consider the case of Bill and Sosume Preston.

"Won't you have a cup of tea?" Mrs. Preston said as she disappeared into the kitchen to put the teakettle on.

It really wasn't a question Stewart decided as his "No, thank you" bounced meaninglessly off the kitchen door. It wasn't that he and his wife Sally wouldn't enjoy a cup of tea with the Prestons, for they most certainly would. Bill and Sosume Preston were a gracious Christian couple who reminded Stewart of his own grandparents. Ordinarily he would have enjoyed visiting very much, but today he had three other church families to visit for the every-member canvass, and he was anxious to get about the church's business. Tea would unnecessarily prolong the visit and maybe even get him (the stewardship chairman) into hot water if he were late to join the other visiting teams back at the church that evening. Stewart reviewed the papers he had brought along. Sally sighed and got settled into the easy chair. Bill failed to hide the smile that was slowly spreading across his face.

As Sosume prepared cups, spoons, tea bags, napkins, and honey, she smiled at the thought of the young couple in their parlor. *The Shipleys are so full of energy and enthusiasm. They're doing a fine job with the high school Sunday School class, and reviving the every-member canvass was their idea, too. I'm glad that they were transferred into the area, and I hope they won't be transferred out too soon. I'm glad to finally have them over. How often I've thought to invite them over for dinner, but I never quite got myself organized for it. Seems like what used to come easy now comes harder. Well, here they are. Let's seize the moment. I can't do everything, but I'll do what I can,* Sosume consoled herself.

"Now as you can see from the first column on this sheet, we will need an increase of about 8 percent in giving—considering inflation and who's died—just to stay even with last year. But as you can see by reviewing the line items on last year's budget, we don't really **do** anything. I mean paying the pastor—whose sermons, by the way, are getting better, I'm sure you will agree—and keeping the doors open are just sunk costs. That's the price we pay to be in business. But the business of the church is ministry. So the second column represents a commitment that starts to mean something. It is an increase in giving of 20 percent but an increase in ministry of 100 percent. It includes remodeling the front half of the basement and opening a drop-in center for teenagers on Friday, Saturday, and Sunday nights each week. The mission committee has done a survey and found that most of the teenagers in town are bored. A supervised drop-in center would give them something positive to do in a healthy environment."

Bill seemed to remember that the Shipleys were on the mission committee, too.

"Supervised, you say." Sosume reflected.

"Definitely. How can we witness if we aren't there? I've drawn up a schedule for each family in the church to take a weekend on a rotating basis. Of course, we wouldn't let you do this cold. There will be plenty of training and review and evaluation sessions, too."

"I see. And what's the third column?" asked Sosume a trifle too pleasantly.

"Ah, that's our challenge budget. That is where we really step on the gas for Christ. Among other things it includes remodeling the back half of the basement into a soup kitchen and emergency shelter. We've done a survey and. . . ."

Sosume admitted to the pastor later that she hadn't heard much of the particulars of the soup kitchen because she was trying to figure out how long a nap she would have to take on Friday and Saturday and Sunday afternoons if she were to stay up with the teenagers until midnight and still get up at the crack of dawn to tend to her chores.

The next thing she remembered was her husband's voice. "Last week I drove my old pickup down to the dealer. The brakes were getting kind of spongy, and I figured mebbe I'd be just as well off trading her in. I found one sitting on the lot with about the right size engine and bed. 'How much?' I says. Well, the salesman got to adding in extra for the leather seats. Extra for the pile carpeting. Extra for the quadraphonic music system. Then he just kind of smiled when I asked him where the rear speakers were. Extra for the chromized wire hubcaps. Finally, he gives me a number with about as many zeroes after it as the national debt. So I says, 'Thank you' and I drive down to Lou's garage and get my brakes redone. I don't need no penthouse on wheels. All I need to do is get from here to there . . . you know what I mean?"

After an awkward silence Stewart assured Bill that he did. Then he asked Bill and Sosume to fill out the pledge card, seal it in the attached envelope, and it would be returned confidentially to the church treasurer and the pastor. Sosume hadn't noticed any change in the sermons. They were about as good as they always were. Stewart was pleased that they wrote a number down so quickly after his final plea for the third column with its 50 percent increase in budget. It even made the tea taste sweeter.

But Stewart's inductive Bible study program had not yet gotten to the verse that says sweet in the mouth, bitter in the stomach. He was quite shocked to learn at the end of the team meeting that evening that Bill and Sosume had actually pledged 50 percent less than last year!

The next day the pastor sat in the parlor sipping tea with the Prestons.

"You know, folks," he chuckled, "if you wanted me to visit, you could've just said so. You didn't have to scare Stewart Shipley half to death, you know."

"I reckon the devil made me do it, Pastor Buck!" said Bill with a broad smile on his broad face. "I just couldn't resist."

"You think Stewart will forgive us when he finds out that we are really going to up our giving by 10 percent?" asked Sosume with more seriousness than Rev. John Bucklin had expected.

"I'm sure he will." Curiosity then got the better of Pastor Buck. "Why did you decide on 10 percent?"

"Well, we could see that 8 percent would keep us even. Ten percent allows us to go forward at a pace we can handle."

"It's not the money," Sosume added. "If we scrimped we could give more still."

"And if an emergency came up, we'd eat crackers to make sure the church pulled through. You know that, Pastor," said Bill.

"It was the idea of why we should give that bothered us. Pastor, you know how much Bill and I do for the Lord, for our church, and for people in town who could use a hand. Why, there isn't a church board or committee that we haven't served on. We've taught Sunday School for generations! We've had teenagers over to our house since our kids were teens and many years after. We've fed needy families, we've 'hired' folks that were down on their luck. We've had families live with us for weeks while they were betwixt and between. But we always figured that was what Christians did. And we did it when it was necessary, when people we knew about were hurting. In the time of need we found the strength to respond.

"The idea that we should give more to the church so that then we could *do* more just strikes us wrong. We are already doing what we can. Even the thought of doing more makes me tired. And our idea of church isn't doing. Church isn't where you get used up. You don't get to heaven in the fast lane. Church is where I can be still and know God. Church is where I can look around on Sunday morning and see Maggie who doesn't sing very well, but never quits trying to get it right. And Old Monty who's been scoutmaster for nearly half a century because he really believes in what God can do with young people. Oh, he's had his disappointments in that regard, but he's had his vindications, too. And how about Vincent? I've never heard him complain about how the church gets left. He knows he can't organize more than a broom and a dustpan at the same time, but he figures his ministry is to help other people do their ministry. And even though Lucretia and I aren't too warmly right now, I know she's half right and she knows I'm half right, and we will patch it together again pretty soon. It just kind of warms my heart, these people do. And they don't have to do anything either, except be who they are by God's grace. That's why we're giving to the first column, Pastor. Sometimes not doing much is still doing a whole lot. And anyhow, I don't go to church to get used up like I said. I go to be with my brothers and sisters and know way down in the bottom of my heart that I am a part of God's family. I hope that's OK with you, Pastor, 'cause that's the way it is."

After inquiring how the brake job was holding up, Pastor Buck went on his way rejoicing.

TWENTY CHARACTERISTICS

THE DEGREE OF "SMALLNESS" OF YOUR CHURCH

Mark each question *a* or *b* according to which is more characteristic of your church. Most churches exhibit some of each dynamic. Mark the one which your church tends to exhibit most.

1. Is your church (a) small in number, or (b) large in number?
2. Have most of the people in your church known each other a relatively (a) short time, or (b) long time?
3. Would you say that those in your church who know one another well have acquired that knowledge (a) through working together at the church for many years, or (b) through intimate sharing/fellowship groups?
4. If a disruptive pastor were let loose on your congregation, would the response of the majority of the people be (a) to look around for a better church, or (b) stick it out and fight for the church?
5. Does your church have a (a) low, or (b) high connection with other churches, community groups, and ecumenical organizations?
6. Does your church see itself as (a) the people, not the building, or (b) the people and the building because the people who built the building are important to us?
7. Is your church (a) more or less self-contained, or is it (b) significantly impacted by the environment?
8. Are the people who are highly valued in your church (a) the young and energetic, the shakers and the movers, or (b) those with gray hair and many years?
9. Do the younger people in your church (a) experience more or less the same activities that the older generation did at their age, or (b) participate in new programs designed for their needs?

10. Is most of the work in your church done (a) by individuals with particular expertise or training, or (b) could it be done by most anyone who would try?

11. Do people know what is going on in your congregation (a) by tuning into the grapevine, or (b) by reading the parish newsletter?

12. (a) Are there a number of layers in your church's organization, or (b) does it run by a fairly simple system?

13. Do people act in the life of the church according to their (a) social position, or (b) duties spelled out in the bylaws?

14. Do people act in order (a) to get things done and change the situation, or (b) to express their feelings about the situation?

15. In committee meetings do people (a) spend two hours talking to get two minutes' work done, or (b) work their way efficiently down the agenda?

16. Are people more motivated (a) to achieve their personal goals, or (b) by the attribution of esteem by the rest of the church?

17. Are people who are respected (a) staid, stable, dependable, but not too creative, or (b) those with charming manners and new ideas?

18. Does your church (a) enact programs to meet conscious needs, or (b) do what it is used to doing?

19. Are new programs in your church (a) seen as a threat to the ordained order, or (b) considered on their merits?

20. Are people called (a) by the names they present, or (b) by nicknames given to them?

(Scoring: Count the number of *a* answers given to the odd-numbered questions. Add this to the number of *b* answers of the even-numbered questions. The closer this total is to 20, the more your church is like a folk society.)

4

But We've Always Done It This Way!

Strategies for Successful Small Church Fund-Raising

Effective stewardship can be accomplished in the small church, but it won't necessarily look like the stewardship in other kinds of churches. Successful fund-raising in the small church will have its specific form and content. It will arise out of the particular life of the small church. In this chapter we will offer nine strategies for successful fund-raising in the small church. If you are a how-to person, this is your chapter.

Small Church as Tribe

As we discussed in the previous chapter, the small church embodies the same social dynamics as the biblical concept of "people," the anthropological ideal type of folk society and the sociological construct Gemeinschaft. Based on these understandings, we can think of the small church as a "tribe." If we make this our operating image of the small church, where does it lead us?

Well, a tribe is composed of people who live in face-to-face relationships. Theirs is a personal existence. They think in terms of the whole social unit and feel their well-being is tied to the well-being of the whole group. Native American tribes speak of a sphere of existence. And this is exactly how the world feels to folk people. It feels whole and integrated, not fractionated and compartmentalized (although it needs to be to some extent). The cast of characters, the rhythm of life, the sense of space and place—all have a wholeness and a sense of fullness and closeness (and to the degree they lack these things, to that extent is there a feeling of lament and loss).

The past is very important to a tribe. The way things have been done is the way things *are* done. The wheel does not have to be reinvented each day or week or for each stewardship drive. The way things have been done is, by and large, the familiar and, therefore, the comfortable way of doing them. Tradition is of major significance to tribal people. And to those who would be chief, understanding the traditions of the group is crucial because it defines the behavioral repertoire available to the group at the present.

The past is also important because it is the context of those people who gave shape to the tribe—the patriarchs (be they male or female). From the vision, sacrifice, heroism, blood, sweat, and tears of our fathers and mothers does the tribe derive its essence today. This can degenerate into ancestor worship, but there is no such thing as tribal life without the memory—the guiding, energizing, and connecting, as well as the restricting memory—of those who have gone before. This feature of tribal life brings together the twin realities of tradition and personalness.

Leadership is exercised in the tribe, usually through patterned behavior—habits. The chief is able to lead by selecting among the behavioral routines of the people the one appropriate for the present need. For example, at various points in time the chief will activate the tribe's ability to hunt large game, prepare for war against a hostile neighbor, or combat illness within the camp. These behavioral sets are not reinvented by the chief; they are selected.

This preference among tribal people for acting along habitual lines has two further implications. Intentionality, rationality, and attribution are not valued in the eyes of the tribe. Life is already dealt with in the total response repertoire of their culture. The culture itself is the tribe's plan for the future since it doesn't see or foresee much difference between tomorrow and yesterday. Changes in the tribe's behavior, then, are unlikely to occur by fiat, but rather must arise "accidentally" from the impetus of life itself. The second implication is that while things that occur regularly are dealt with (or thought to be) in the preconscious, unself-reflective culture of the tribe, a perceived crisis allows the possibility of change. Incremental changes in the environment are unlikely to be registered as threats (situations demanding attention) by a tribal people. But massive and immediate discontinuity is the occasion for new behavior for tribes. Our rational society prefers change by evolution, not revolution. But whenever a tribal chief can say, in the words of Chester A. Riley, "What a revolting development this is," the situation is ripe for change.

Strategies

With these characteristics in mind, how will wise small church leaders go about raising funds? I would suggest nine strategies—none radically new, but all flowing from the life dynamics of the small church-tribe.

The first strategy of successful fund-raising in the small church is to utilize the concern for the well-being of the congregation.

One of the greatest motivations for members giving to their small church (usually the smaller the church, the greater this motivation) is the desire to see the church they value and love healthy. "Who among you if your child asks for a fish would give him a stone?" asks Jesus. The family member who feels love, ownership, and responsibility toward the other members of the family and the family unit as a whole is highly motivated to provide for them to the limits of his or her ability. Tied to the family's well-being is the individual's own sense of well-being. "Whatever it takes" is a common expression in my small community. Whatever it takes to ensure our health and well-being we will do.

This same feeling/identity/motivation is at work in the small church. In some small churches it is the force that keeps the church going and the doors open against major odds. In other small churches it lies undervalued and underdeveloped. But this is the starting point for all financial giving to Christ's church, I believe: the reality that we are one in Christ and given life, meaning, and purpose in relation to God's people. It is the sentiment that Ruth expressed to Naomi: "Where you go I will go, and where you lodge I will lodge; your people shall be my people, and your God my God. . ." (Ruth 1:16).

Doug Walrath relates a story about how his first parish, a rural parish, finished each year in the black. The elders met at the end of the year. They listened to the report of the treasurer. It was just one figure—the number of dollars they were in the red. Then they went around the table. Each man offered an amount against the deficit. This continued until the deficit was made up. Some years it really squeezed these farmers to bail out the church. But, of course, they never thought of it that way. They were acting to insure that what was valuable and important to them survived.

The small church is important to its members. There they find their faith deepened and the bonds of love strengthened. In raising funds for the continuance of the ministry of the small church, it is this reality that is foundational. How might one proceed in light of this? *The Every Member Un-Canvass*[1] is an example of using the well-being—the joy, growth, and love—of the whole congregation as a motivational impetus for responsible giving.

The Every Member Un-Canvass, at first look, does not seem much different from the old Every Member Canvass approach. It is a stewardship drive including administration (chairman, helpers, schedule), communication from the church to its members (mailings, sermons, and bulletin information), and a call to commitment (pledge cards and follow-up phone calls and visits). But it differs at some very important points that radically change its validity and results. The Un-Canvass approach originated in an Episcopal parish in Indianapolis, Indiana. Frank Ogelsby, the Un-Canvass chairman, writes of previous Every Member Canvasses: "We got the job done. However, we always caused frowns, growls, boos, hisses

. . . just by mentioning 'Every Member Canvass'. . . . [Now with the Every Member Un-Canvass] *best of all* a whole new receptive attitude to our Canvass has been established."

The Un-Canvass also reverses the idea of when to use individual or group approaches. A typical large church canvass utilizes a sizeable committee to make individual calls on parish members. The Un-Canvass has one trusted, committed, and respected church member do all the asking. And no individual home calls are made (unless requested by the family). Instead, all the asking is done once, in the context of the entire church family.

The last point of difference may be the most significant. Church members are asked to pledge not simply to fulfill their Christian duty, not simply to allow the church to run or expand its ministry, but out of the sheer joy of their common life! How does the Un-Canvass work? A camera bug in the congregation is asked to take slides of "everything that moves" in the church over the course of the year—including, and especially, shots of each person, as well as all events in the church's year. On Un-Canvass Sunday the pastor preaches a stewardship sermon, the congregation then shares a brunch together. Then on comes the slide show. As people see their loved ones, remember joyous occasions, and laugh at their foibles, they realize anew the centrality of the church to what is meaningful and important in life for them. Then the chairman makes a pitch and collects the completed pledge cards.

That's it? That's it (except for some follow-up phone calls)! And the results? Frank Ogelsby figures his church is way ahead. Individual pledges, total amount pledged, and pledges fulfilled have all increased for three years running. And the Brunch–Slide Show is so much more fun, easier to do, and more highly valued than a home-visit-type canvass.

Another stewardship program that has been used successfully in some small churches is *Adventure in Thanks/Giving.*[2] This program requires the leadership of three laypersons and the pastor over a period of six weeks. During this period, biblical stewardship is emphasized in preaching and teaching. Individuals are encouraged to manage wisely all of their God-given resources, such as money, time, talents, and creation itself. Each member of the congregation is asked to share "three wishes" for the life and work of the church. A Thanks/Giving Dinner is held where the collated three wishes of the congregation are presented. Each member is then challenged to make an estimate of giving for the following year.

The second strategy for successful fund-raising in the small church is to utilize the congregation's life as an instrument.

The social dynamics of a small church are perceived as an end, not a means, by the members. The web of relationships is satisfying and rewarding in and of itself. It is fun and enjoyable. It provides a major part of both the context and the content of the interpersonal life of the church members. These interpersonal bonds are some of the most important building blocks of the world of small church people. To build them up and live them out is both enjoyable and "right" to a small church person.

Contrast this attitude to that of a very successful church planter with whom I recently conversed. I was quite intrigued by his vocation, so I asked many questions. He willingly shared both his joys and his difficulties in getting a new church started. One of his major difficulties was in achieving "decultivation." It seems that in the early stages of starting a new congregation he would spend much time in "cultivating" a few prospective families. These people would come to know the church planter intimately. They enjoyed him, they liked him, and in a true interpersonal sense, they came to love him. And that was the problem. The love that jelled this nucleus could prohibit the church planter from cultivating the next round of prospective members. In order to proceed with establishing a church, he had to decultivate the first group without disenfranchising them! It was tricky business, for they always thought that they were valued for themselves. Of course, as children of God, they are inherently valuable. But to the church planter as church planter their value had now shifted.

They were now an interpersonal liability, entangling him and interfering with his next level of ministry. Their value now was essentially structural—providing a base upon which to build. He lamented to me how they never seemed to understand this.

Small church people wouldn't understand this man and his ministry. For small church people, interpersonal relationships—with their joys and frustrations and world defining characteristics—are an end, not a means. The fellowship (sharing experiences, making of memories, the fun of working together, of just being together) is a very potent motivation. This is the stuff of the small church world. And almost any excuse to engage in it is responded to with enthusiasm and interest. In this sense it is a ministry to the whole body to organize fund-raisers!

Two friends of mine worship in a small church in the hills of Pennsylvania. The church has very limited financial resources, so every project they take on depends on some form of miracle for its accomplishment. Maybe that is why every year when I see them again my friends have some wonderful story to tell me of God's activity in their congregation. This year's tale is about handbells. The church had decided to start a handbell choir. But how to raise the money necessary? They considered many ideas. They tried various approaches. And then they hit upon it—a silent auction!

"A silent auction?" I asked, straining my imagination to conceive of an auction in silence. I could not in my wildest fantasies conceive of a small church gathering together and keeping still!

"Oh, no!" they chuckled. "The group was noisy as ever. It was the bids that were silent." They went on to explain that items and services had been solicited in advance. People gave all kinds of things—fruit baskets from an orchard owner, prints by an artist, an appliance repair call from a Mr. Fix-it type, usable items no longer needed by their owners, and so forth. The items were all displayed in the church hall, and the services were described. Then opportunity was given to place written bids under any and all items. The whole church had a grand time as they circulated about, talking with one another, oohing and aahing over unusual things, catching up on one another's lives, talking about everything except the bids they were placing on the items. Then the highest bid on each item was listed on a blackboard, and a second round of bidding ensued. Now people knew who had bid what, who was going to get the item if no other bids were made, who was going to lose out unless another bid was offered. And so a second round of bids was placed. As people bid against one another, subtly or obviously, enjoying the competitiveness as well as the conversation, the fun was heightened. When the bidding was finished, the items were awarded amidst great noise, disappointment, cheering, and booing, and general joy and happiness. The total receipts revealed that the handbells could now be ordered. Coffee and refreshments ended a most joyous and productive evening.

Releasing the joy and fun inherent in the social connections of the small church can indeed be a significant fund-raising approach.

The third strategy of successful fund-raising in the small church is to utilize patterned behaviors already within the memory and activity repertoire of the congregation. *Or, to put it simply, habits can be profitable!*

A Higgledy-Piggledy type of organization proceeds rationally to achieve a profit. The market is *analyzed*. Goals are *specified*. Alternatives are *weighed*. Resources are *allocated*. Progress is *monitored*. And, if management is really sharp, procedures and personnel will be changed every few years simply to avoid habituation of behavior! Rational organizations recognize the human tendency to form habits, so they act against it.

In a Ralph-type organization, on the other hand, habits are not viewed as negative, but as reality. A tribe does not operate out of its head—rationally. On a group level, it operates out of the common understanding and world view that holds the group together, that is, its culture. And individually it operates out of its reservoir of learned behaviors—habit. When I walk,

I do not analyze the particular muscle movements and their sequence and then trigger them at the appropriate moment. My conscious level decides to walk, and all the behaviors, their timing, and sequence automatically kick in because they are "written" in the fiber of my nerves and muscles. It is second nature to me. It is an activity that is patterned in the very stuff that is me. My wife says I have a distinctive gait. Who cares? It gets me where I'm going. I suppose I could change my gait, but why should I? It gets me where I'm going. And it allows me to meditate, commune, or mellow out *while* I am getting there. The utilization of patterned behavior is very efficient because it allows a second simultaneous activity. Rational behavior is inefficient and unrealistically reductionistic because one can only do one thing at a time. We have a blast with fund-raisers in my parish because we are not totally preoccupied with who does what when. We pretty much know all that. So we are free to fellowship together and enjoy the experience. If someone came up with a fund-raising program for our church that eliminated the need for fund-raising projects, I would say, "Get thee behind me, Satan." The simultaneous second activity (fellowship) contributes as much if not more to the well-being of the parish as the funds raised!

I shared this concept with a colleague who did not agree with me. She said, "Oh, yes, we had our annual fair, but I dreaded it. All the hostilities that lay dormant in the parish all year came out as if on cue during the fair." I don't buy her disagreement because it seems a classic case of patterned behavior, so patterned that even the emotions and the bickering that were not exhibited all year(!) were part of the script of the annual fair. Maybe this is a good time to mention that small church nature can be fallen or whole just as human nature can be godly or sinful. The point is that its nature determines *how* one ministers. One ministers differently to a tree or a person. So, too, ministry is different in a large and a small church. But the claim is not being made that all small churches are righteous by virtue of being small, only that they have the capacity to be.

A Sunday afternoon drive through new-fallen snow brought me to a small church in western Vermont to lead a workshop. The pastor and lay people of the host church greeted me and the other participants warmly. In the course of our discussions together, I asked about the signboard announcing a turkey dinner that Friday night. "Oh, we've put on these fund-raising dinners for years and years," I was answered.

"Got the system down, huh?" I observed.

"Yep," said the new pastor, "when they get going, get out of the kitchen!" He looked like he knew whereof he spoke.

"If this is such a tradition," I innocently inquired, "how come the signboard is brand spanking new—nicely done, too?"

Well, a bit of a pause occurred, the interpersonal equivalent of the moistened finger raised to sense the wind. Which way was this guy blowing? Apparently they sensed a good wind, that I could be trusted with their story, and so it came out. For years, as a congregation, they had supplemented their meager income through dinners for the public. Good food at a good price for a good cause. These dinners became a way of life in the parish. The people became quite expert in the production of dinners, and they were proud of it. But then hard times came. Church strife. Aging process. Increasingly mobile community. The dinners, along with lots of other things at the church, became history. Then a new pastor came, a wise old man. "Tell me," he said, "'bout the good old days." Time and again the dinners came up almost as a symbol of the strength of the parish in former days. "Well, the kitchen's still here," he mused. "Enough of you are still here. People still need to eat around here. What hindereth us?"

Overnight the congregation shed twenty years. They cranked up those ovens, just like before. They set the tables, just like before. They opened the doors and spread the word, just like before. And just like before, the people started coming and coming again and coming to every dinner these folk had the energy to put on. No market research. No resource analysis. No procedure manual delegating the work. How to do a dinner was part of the very fiber of the people. They had done it so many times before that even a lull of decades couldn't erode the habit! All they really needed was the OK to be themselves and a "chief" who believed in them and their habits. He gives us all advice about patterned behavior: "When they get going, get out of the kitchen!" Patterned behavior: use it for fund-raising. It can be habit forming!

The fourth strategy of successful fund-raising in the small church is to appeal to the personal and the proximate.

When I shop at our regional version of Higgledy-Piggledy, I really appreciate the check-out girl's attempt to be friendly. It makes the whole exchange more pleasant. But it also underscores the essentially impersonal nature of the encounter. Now, with UPC marking and teenage employees, I not only feel that the whole encounter could be done by robots, but in fact is being done by robots. And that includes the robotic, impersonalness that the situation calls forth in me.

Our town's version of Ralph's, on the other hand, has two check-out ladies most of the year. Both are affiliated with our church. So every trip to buy groceries also includes the latest exchange in our respective lives, comments on what's new at the church and in town. On occasion, the conversation is of such significance that I am all the way out to my car before I realize I left the bag of groceries at the counter!

The business enterprise uses persons to accomplish its material goals. That is its legitimate nature. The family, the clan, the tribe, and the small church, in contrast, use the material in the service of the personal. That is its legitimate nature. Some people are motivated to support the church as an abstract obligation. Some people are motivated to support the church program as a specific good. But small church people are usually motivated to support the church because in the people and relationships of the church they find life. Fund-raising efforts in the small church should not avoid a call to individual faithfulness to the church generic, nor should it avoid a call to be supportive of the ministry activities of the church. But usually more potent than these appeals is the appeal to the personal dimension.

In a neighboring state, there is a small church pastored by a colleague of mine. The men of the church have for many years been involved in a program of renovation of their fellowship hall. They would become inspired, make a burst of progress, weary and quit. And there things would stand for another "thirty-eight years until the angel of the Lord troubled the waters." The pastor wondered if he would ever see the end of the work and the full use of the hall. But into this cyclical yet static situation two events were brought to bear. One happened fifty years previously, and the second one hundred years previously! Fifty years ago a member of the church had moved a building from a remote location to abut the sanctuary. This building became the fellowship hall of the congregation, and the cost of the moving was donated to the church by that member. It was a helpful and generous deed and well appreciated by the congregation. Over the years the hall added significantly to the life and well-being of the parish. The second event was the impending one-hundredth birthday of that very same gentleman. A member of the church reaching one hundred years of age—something to celebrate! The celebration was to take place in the church hall—the very hall that this man had donated. The men could not bear the thought of thanking the man for providing their hall in its present condition. So inspiration hit again. But this time it was sustained by the realization of the meaning the finished hall would have to the gentleman who was responsible for it in the first place. The men kept at it, buying materials, hammering, sawing, painting, cleaning until the job was done. And done in time to celebrate with someone very special to them.

Now, granted, not too much fund-raising was done—just enough for the materials. But resources were released. Energy was given, sustained, and well rewarded with the joy of making a loved one happy. Sometimes small churches don't need to raise funds if they can raise the necessary resources in other forms—elbow grease, material gifts, advice, and counsel. A small church that will accept only money is unnecessarily limiting what God is sending its way. Since the small church lives and moves and has its being on the personal level and is highly motivated by the persons and relations that comprise its social fabric, frequently people will respond by giving personally as well as financially. It may be a gift of time, energy, expertise, just being present, encouragement, advice, exhortation, and so forth. But whatever form it takes, if it is the sincere gift of a person, it is a blessing from the Lord!

The fifth strategy of successful fund-raising in the small church is to utilize accidents as if they were planned.

For the Higgledy-Piggledy manager the worst sin, next to running in the red, is to let oneself be surprised. One plans. One monitors. And one adjusts. But one never gets surprised. For to be surprised by events is to have lost control. And in this rational scheme of things, to be out of control is to experience hell.

But for a tribal people, that which is unplanned and unforeseen has an entirely different role and valuation. It may be viewed negatively as a disruption or positively as an item of interest and fascination. But accidents are not believed to be accidental. They are held to be part of the Great Intention, and therefore a godsend. In the poignant movie *The Gods Must Be Crazy*, a bush pilot throws an empty Coke bottle out of his airplane. It lands near a tribe of people of the African bush. The rest of the movie is the story of their trying to make sense of this object descended from the skies. First they find some positive uses for it in food preparation. Then it causes disruption and hostility as tribesmen argue over it. Finally they determine that the gods must be crazy to be doling out gifts such as this. The movie end with the chief returning the bottle to the gods. Since the tribe cannot register the possibility of an accident, and since the bottle caused nothing but strife, the tribesmen are forced to conclude that indeed the gods intended it but that they are nuts.

In the rational mentality of the Higgledy-Piggledy manager,

accidents (unplanned and unpredicted events) are problematic because they are outside the will (plan, goals, strategies) of the organization and/or its leaders. But in the folk mentality, accidents are seen as a good because they indicate that an intention greater than theirs is working out its purpose. Accidents are, then, a point of connection between us and God and as such motivate a God-ward response. Fund-raisers in the small church should be ever sensitive to parlay accidental events into movement toward God's kingdom.

A colleague of mine pastors a small church in the Wyalusing Valley of Pennsylvania. They were faced with the enviable problem of what to do with their Sunday School. Over the preceding years enrollment had inched up and up, and now the Sunday School faced an undeniable shortage of space. But what to do? Re-utilize the existing space? Remodel and re-configure the present classrooms? Expand into the "attic." One by one each alternative proved inadequate as a solution. Adding Sunday School rooms was the only workable plan, but the layout of the church lot yielded no satisfactory direction. At that very moment the owner of the property next door—an ancient, encumbered, and rundown hotel—announced that insurance rates, indebtedness, and other problems were forcing him to bail out. If the church would pay off the tax liens, the property was theirs. And that property was the ideal direction for the new wing! Some coincidence, huh? What a wonderful accident. Well, that good Presbyterian congregation didn't quite see it that way. To them it was much more. "It was a sign," the pastor reflected. "It was nothing less than providence," the people said. Their previous rational solution to their space shortage had been only moderately supported, but now the obvious solution was perceived as a divinely ordained activity, and the commitment of the congregation to it soared. But wait, there's more. The church paid off the back taxes, bulldozed the unsafe building, drew up plans, and got contractor bids. Then they sat down stunned. The bids were double the original estimates. How could they do it? Was God really in it after all? A meeting was called to decide go or no go. And if go, how? Shortly before the meeting the pastor received legal correspondence. An elderly lady who had died weeks before had, unbeknownst to the congregation, willed a sizeable gift for the congregation's use. Not enough to finish the construction, but enough that the congregation could carry the ball the rest of the way! Surprise? Coincidence? Accident? I suppose. But to those in the congregation, two stone tablets wouldn't have been greater evidence of God's living and motivating presence. They gave. They built. And they praised. But remember, they had the spiritual smarts to see what was unplanned and unpredictable from a human point of view as planned all along by the eternal will of God. This was God's doing, and their contributions now put them squarely in the center of God's perfect will.

The sixth strategy of successful small church fund-raising is to recognize the power of a crisis to generate a response.

This is not to advocate the manufacturing of crises to order. But it is to suggest that a crisis now and again is much like an accident only worse, that is, better, in motivating a small church to respond! No organization, whether it is rationally or socially structured, desires to have a crisis. But rational organizations seem to go to great lengths to avoid even the appearance of one. Instead, they strive to give the feeling that, yes, management is truly in charge. A socially structured organization such as the small church finds, rather, that an occasional crisis can be very healthy. For it is in the midst of a crisis that new ideas can be entertained and new behaviors successfully introduced to a tribal-type group.

I am pleased to report that I once turned a moderate problem into a full-scale crisis in our parish precisely so that it would generate a response of greater faithfulness in our congregation's fund-raising! Prior to that occasion we had very little concern for our church building. Maintenance problems were dealt with in the cheapest and quickest manner. It would have been easier to have the Pope come and preach to us about the positives of ordaining women than to get our trustees to support a fund drive! But then one December we found ourselves way over budget for fuel oil. Our drafty, uninsulated, and oversized building provided a bottomless pit for heating oil, but up until then we had somehow avoided the inevitable. Now our luck had run out. Or had it? We could have gritted our teeth and gone on. I could have waited until after the first of the year to order our next load. I could have, but I didn't. I was determined to bring things to a head, to make a problem into a crisis, in order that we might gain the vision and the will to address the issue. So I ordered yet another load of fuel oil in late December and made an issue of the overage at our congregation's annual business meeting in early January. The dollars spent on fuel oil shocked the people. A committee was formed. A report received. A fund-raising drive started.

The next five plus years saw us raise more than $200,000. We put in new windows, insulated, replaced the heating system, and so forth. Still we fell $35,000 short. So we must keep on keeping on. But now our building is usable, comfortable, and energy efficient. A crisis, now and then, can be healthy for the small church.

The seventh strategy of successful fund-raising in the small church is to communicate more in terms of the past than the future.

"What have you done for me lately?" or more accurately, "What are you going to do for me tomorrow?" is the basis of valuation in the Higgledy-Piggledy organizations of our society. In such entities everything is aimed toward tomorrow. Goals, quotas, profits are all intentions regarding the future. The future is their focus. This is what makes them so potent in our economy. People are important to them, but only insofar as they can positively affect the future.

The tribe, the folk society, the Ralphs of this world, and the small church don't seem to think in terms of tomorrow. Yesterday is where their focus is. What is important is what has already happened: the people who anchor our lives by their lifelong commitment and the circumstances that make up "the good old days." What is good about tomorrow is that it holds the promise of feeling like yesterday. This valuation of the past is what makes these social units so enduring in our society.

The small church is not typically motivated to charge into the future. It is not "greedy for the future." What is motivating and energizing is the past—its ideals, its memories, its overall sense of being "right." Whether this kind of past ever really existed is both debatable and irrelevant. There is something in the folk mentality, maybe even something in the very neural structure of our memories, that motivates tribal people to value the past and act in concert with it. This reality can either be resisted or used to advantage for fund-raising in the small church.

Painting in broad strokes, it is accurate to say that small church people value the past. This orientation colors much, if not all, of small church life. Now this perspective impacts fund-raising on two levels: the motivational and the mechanical. The desire to return to "the good old days" is highly motivating for small church people. And the memories of the past provide much grist for the small church fund-raising mill. These two dimensions were embodied in my church's renovation fund drive which I mentioned in the preceding strategy.

Our fund drive chairman, Brad, was very wily in his pitches regarding the drive. To those in the community at large, the business community, and our visitors, Brad stressed the impact of the church's ministries on the well-being of the community as a whole. Their gifts to the drive would result in a (future) increase of services back to the community. However, to the church membership the appeal was different. Though the dollars from whatever source would accomplish the same renovations, the renovations had a different meaning to those inside the organization. To those outside the church, the changes would improve the future service of the church to the community. To those inside the church, the renovations were to *correct for the deviations* of time. So the appeal to church members was an appeal to restore—to get the church back to when the furnace worked right, to when the Sunday School had adequate space, to get us back to when things felt right. The fund drive was a movement of restoration, to restore the form of the building in which so many significant memories reside. And, of course, Brad wasn't afraid to claim the next step, too. If our children are to have the same quality of memories that we do, the building must be in good repair for them as it was for us. Utilizing the past in this way, Brad came to the congregational meeting on whether to proceed with the drive armed with over twenty-three thousand dollars in pre-pledges!

But long drives bog down. The scale of ours practically guaranteed that there would be periods of little or no advance. During one such period a group of church leaders were debating how to get back on track when we got off on a tangent, not untypically! "Oh, that reminds me," led to a story of the hurricane forty-five years before that destroyed the fishing fleet forever and agriculture for years on our island. While I was enjoying the reminiscing and the respite from our heavy agenda, I noticed Brad's eyes had glazed over. He had made some connection and was spinning it out in his mind. Then he spoke and our "Heritage Dinners" were born. (Our first three dinners were on the anniversaries of hurricanes, shipwrecks, and fires, respectively—so they were dubbed "Disaster Dinners," a moniker we are trying valiantly to suppress!)

"What's a Heritage Dinner?" you ask. Well, a Heritage Dinner is first of all a dinner. We serve a multicourse, sitdown, limited-seating meal—choice of steak or lobster—at a significant price (although less than most restaurants in town). We pride ourselves on our old-fashioned quality and portions and our homemade desserts. After the meal, the guests proceed to the sanctuary for a panel discussion of one aspect of our heritage. Some of our older townspeople are invited to be on the panel. They share artifacts, descriptions, explanations, genealogies, and stories that could go on all night. The Historical Society pitches in with a visual display (which I invariably utilize for my children's sermon the next day). I wish space permitted a description of the dynamics of the occasion and an account of the energy that is released. Suffice to say that people go home thrilled to have remembered their past. And so far Brad has netted (the last dinner was on fishing) almost eight thousand dollars for our renovations! Our Heritage Dinners combine past and repast in a way that is psychologically and financially profitable for the church. How *you* do it will be different, of course. But don't overlook the past as a primary means of financing your future!

The eighth strategy of successful fund-raising in the small church is to utilize memorial gifts.

Memories are very important in the small church. We have already noted the power of history to motivate small church people. And we have noted the significance of personalness in the life of the small church. Memorials are a means of bringing together persons and the past in such a way as to release resources for the future.

The persons of the past are orienting and motivating to "folk" people. The Bible spends pages and pages relaying genealogies that seem meaningless to us today but that were crucially important to the original readers, for it placed the narrative in social history and defined the kind of response incumbent upon the descendants. All tribal societies give a significant place to those who have gone before. Whatever Ralph Junior does—innovative or conservative—he does in the presence of the memory of how Ralph Senior would have done it. Folk people, small church people, do not know what it means to live without the "great cloud of witnesses."

Many pastors find this debilitating. They are tired of hearing how Aunt Florence did it or what Captain Anderson (dead four decades) would have felt about it. And sometimes it is wearisome. But it can also be a lifesaver for small church fund-raising. People, small church people especially, will frequently give, and sometimes quite generously, to keep the memory of a loved one alive.

I relearned the power of this motivation just a few weeks ago in regard to my church's quest to obtain handbells. We had been given a most sizeable and generous memorial gift toward the purchasing of handbells. This gift took us to the halfway point of the cost of a two-octave set. I was pleased, our choir director tickled, our organist thrilled. But for some reason the drive seemed ill-fated. We publicized it in our bulletins and newsletter. We talked it up at worship and other gatherings. Everyone agreed it was a great idea. But no one contributed. Since we were struggling with our operating budget, I just let this over-and-above project ride. But after weeks went by, it started to become awkward and embarrassing. The original donor became discouraged. Then our organist, who had researched the types and costs of the bells, informed me of a projected price increase. Do we have enough for a down payment? Maybe, but with no money coming in, it would be foolhardy to order at this time. What to do? How to get off dead center? I knew the donor would be pleased, the congregaton delighted, the choir excited when we got the handbells. When . . . maybe I should say "if."

Into this mood the original donor let fall an idea. "Tony, if it makes a difference, let people know they can give in memory of whomever they like." Click. Right! A quick call to our organist revealed the average cost per bell. The next Sunday at worship I announced that individual bells could be given in memory of a loved one, and I gave the details. Then it happened. By the time I had finished greeting everyone at worship's end, enough money had been pledged to cover the second octave. By week's end enough memorials had been donated to purchase a three-octave set! I was both humbled and awed by the simplicity and rapidity of the solution.

My mother once told me, "Anthony, if you have the choice of making money or making memories, choose memories. Then when you get to the end of life you will have something solid to hold onto." She thinks like a small church person. Memorials are to the small church what memories are to the person: something solid, something grounding, something meaningful. Of course, she's wrong, too. Money and memories are not always alternatives. Memories can be money in the small church.

The ninth strategy of successful fund-raising in the small church is to utilize a fund-raising specialty.

Generic fund-raising has never turned me on. I get my denomination's packet. I've written to stewardship program publishers. From each I have received some very good stuff. But I have yet to get excited about it, I suppose for the very reason that it was produced to appeal to many churches. It just seemed so. . . homogenized!

When I enter a Higgledy-Piggledy, I know what I am going to find. This makes it less threatening, but more boring, too. I actually enjoy popping into the "Ralph's Pretty Goods" of our country when I travel, precisely because I never know exactly what I am going to find. Each one has something different and personal about it.

Taken as a category, tribal people are incredibly rich in diversity. Each tribe has its own dialect, stories, clothing, culture, and technology. Two tribes claiming descent from the same ancestor, living in the same environment, and having the same resources available to them, may build their culture, technology, and way of life in ways that bear virtually no similarity. These peculiarities, specialities, define who they are. Their identity is wrapped up in their differences. Sometimes these differences are deliberately utilized to reinforce identity, such as the emblem that Arab tribes used to precede them into battle. At the same time, this emblem symbolized the tribe and differentiated it from its enemy tribe. Other times these differences arise naturally out of the way life is resolved by the tribe. To the tribe it is unthinkable to attempt to compromise away these differences. The particular way they do things is who they are. To tamper with this is to defile the integrity of the tribe.

This truth seems to be lost to the church in general. Models of faithfulness in one setting are held up for emulation when instead they should serve as inspiration. Small churches are directed to act like large churces. Churches here (rural, urban) are told to look like churches there (suburban). Yet God made churches just like God made people and tribes: each different, each specific, each with its own integrity.

For fund-raising this means that each church has to work out its own salvation with fear and trembling. Yes, we should listen to one another, learn from one another, and look to one another for encouragement and insight. But we each have to proceed on the basis of who we are and work it out our own way. Each church will then develop its own style of fund-raising. Some will be loose about it; some uptight. Some will preach tithing from the rooftops; some will lubricate the church gears with elbow grease. Some will do a bit of everything; some will fine tune one or two methods.

Some churches will parlay specific fund-raising ideas into their identities as faithful congregations of Christ. Not all churches go this route, but let those that do rejoice in it. I have mentioned the church in Vermont that found financial resurgence in a good habit. After many years they still remembered how to put on a great feed as a fund-raiser. When they got back into the swing of it, some connections started to be made. Two members noticed how much good food was left over (ordered so as not to run out). Two remembered how many able-bodied people were at the old-age home up the road. Somebody else remembered that two plus two equals four, and he invited all the folks from the home who could walk to come down to the church for dinner—no charge. And they came. And the committee realized that they had opened the doors to a whole new ministry possibility. Will the church find mission in their meals? Will the church people make a habit of going to the home in between meals to say "hi" to their new friends? Don't know yet. But they could become the church that literally ate their way to heaven!

There's another church in Vermont that has already turned a specialty fund-raiser into their witness. The church folk put on a "game" dinner each fall. People come from miles around— even busloads from Canada—to enjoy this great and unusual feast. One, two, three seatings are necessary. The people of the church work like crazy to pull it off. In one fell swoop they put their church in the black. It's OK to be known as The Game Church, but the pastor got to wondering if the evening could have a spiritual aspect. So he invited those awaiting the next seating into the sanctuary to be comfortable while waiting. Then, to pass the time, he started sharing some of the history of the church and the dinner and so on. And, oh, yes, just before it was time to go into the hall to be served, he offered a blessing over the food and the guests. Now it's not how Billy Graham does evangelism, but it is how that church shares a word about Christ. It's their fund-raising specialty. It's their special ministry. It's who they are and how they do it. God bless 'em!

Conclusion

In this chapter we sought to show how certain fund-raising approaches flowed from the nature of the small church as a folk society, a tribal-like group. Wherever possible we also attempted to describe the opposite or inappropriate approach for small churches. It is necessary to speak a few words of caution at this point. The first is that this list is undoubtedly not exhaustive. It represents the author's best "wisdom" to this point. But it is hoped that other approaches can be added from the front line of small church life. Second, these nine strategies are not to be understood as radically new or distinct. In fact, if the author's premise that the folk society is the most appropriate model of the small church is substantially accurate, then these approaches must be both time tested and interrelated, for such is the folk society. A fund-raising approach in your church may simultaneously combine two or more of these nine strategies. The more strategies represented in an activity, the more powerful that activity as a motivator. And third, not all of these approaches will fit every small church. I have had pastors tell me that memorials just don't fly in their churches. OK, so I'm not hitting on all cylinders for you. This list is like life. Take what works for you and leave the rest for the next person. No, I'm not giving refunds. To risk is to live.

Weathering the Storm

Paying the Minister

For many small churches the challenge of keeping the ship of church afloat is not on the order of fixing a small leak in the hull. Rather, it is on the order of weathering a raging tempest. Three storms have struck the small church. Help is needed right now if these crises are to be weathered. The first crisis concerns how to pay the minister. The second crisis is how to maintain the church building. The third crisis regards how the mission of Christ can be undertaken by the small church. The next three chapters will consider tacks that will help us weather these storms.

In these chapters we will attempt to "prime your pump" in response to these storms. A bucketful of possible responses will be presented. These are not new or magical solutions. Rather, it is hoped that surveying the list will cause a connection to be made, an insight obtained, a realization of "Hey, that's us; that would fit our way of working." It is my hope that a light bulb will go on in your spiritual imagination! But if it does, consider your work just begun. In a rationally structured organization, the idea leads to the action. But in a socially structured organization, like the small church, the idea leads nowhere unless it can be embodied in the life and behavioral pattern of the group.[1] Nevertheless, a "light shining in the darkness" can produce hope and enthusiasm.

Surveying the Clergy Situation

The biggest perceived need in many small churches is the obtaining of qualified clergy. The biggest obstacle to the obtaining of qualified clergy is financial. The situation has become more problematic over the past few decades. This is so for many reasons. One: The small church has fewer internal resources today. Doug Walrath claims that the small church is more than just small; it is getting smaller. As the "old faithful" die, they are replaced by others, but not in equal number. Hence, the membership rolls are shrinking year by year. Through our total population is larger, it is also more secular and less "Christian." So fewer, proportionally, avail themselves of church involvement. Those that do frequently prefer the electronic church or the largely programmatic church to the small church. And then there are simply fewer people in open country and village settings. The national population seems to be concentrating in an urban, suburban, and exurban band along each coast. Two: Economic factors have hurt the small church's ability to compete in the clerical market. Scores of thousands of small churches find themselves in economically depressed regions. The unemployment rate in these areas is higher, and those people who are employed usually earn less than others in comparable jobs in more prosperous areas. There is less money in general and less money in the church as well. Also, inflation has increased the cost of services required by the church more than the average income of many church members has increased. Those church members who find themselves with adequate financial resources often choose to spend their time (and their money) vacationing and visiting their grown children and their grandchildren— laudable actions individually, but hurtful to the fabric of small church life. Three: Large numbers of "trained" clergy nowadays either won't or can't serve small churches at base level (or lower) salaries. That they won't is evidenced by the surfeit of people with degrees from Protestant seminaries simultaneously co-existing with thousands of unfilled rural pastorates. Is it a case of "how your gonna keep 'em down on the farm after they've seen Paree?" or is it that the suburban background of most seminary graduates ill equips them for small town/small church ministry? Whatever the cause, the result is large numbers of empty pulpits. That they can't fill these vacancies is evidenced by the level of indebtedness of many seminary graduates, a significant number of whom are single parents. For these people to accept a call to a small church is to face, not simply poverty, but bankruptcy. Four: Projected retirement patterns in some mainline denominations as compared to ordination rates indicate that soon it will be a seller's market for clergy.

The situation is not rosy, but it is not without hope, either. For convenience we can approach our discussion of paying the pastor by working our way down the apparent sequence of preferences of small churches regarding their pastoral situation. I repeat, we are using this approach for convenience, not because I feel this sequence is biblical, faithful, or helpful. I have grave doubts as to that.

First Preference: Our Own, Full-Time, Trained Clergy

This option, though highly preferred by most churches, is becoming less and less possible. As most denominations raise the base level of salary for full-time clergy and as the number of clergy available shrinks, the chances of any one church obtaining its own personal pastor is decreasing. However, the odds are improved if the congregation will consider female, second-career, or retired clergy.

The Nurturing Leadership Style

Many small churches are looking for a Moses to be their next clergyman. Their new pastor should be a charismatic leader with a great vision of God's future, who will lead them into the Promised Land. "O God," they pray, "send us a messiah quick to deliver us from the land of marginality. Let us be healthy and strong as we used to be. As for me and my congregation, we will promise to pay him the denomination's minimum salary for one year, so as to give him enough time to fix all our problems. Just as you once raised up a Moses for your people, send to us a new Moses. Amen."

This prayer reflects an attitude sincerely, if unreflectively, held by many small church people. Unfortunately, they overlook what happened when God actually did send a Moses. First of all, he was rejected. "Who made you lord and master over us?" Second, he was continuously angry with his followers. Someone once quipped that Moses would have been better off if God had given him two aspirin tablets instead of the two stone tablets! Third, the people were never happy with his leadership. They grumbled and groaned for forty years. And, maybe most significant, they all died before they could see any positive results. The attitude "If only we had a Moses for a pastor" is an unhealthy one. The hope for a magical messiah must die if a small church is to move toward health. Leadership that is alongside (not above) and nurturing (not dominating) is healthy small church leadership.

A recent letter to the Alban Institute's *Action-Information Journal*, responding to Celia Hahn's description of male and female leadership styles, described the leadership style of the letter writer's friend and colleague. This friend is a "successful parish minister." His leadership style is "inclusive, connective, receptive, patient, humorous, and above all, effective." The writer says, "I would call his style feminist."[2] That letter got me to thinking. Isn't it the qualities of nurturance that a healthy small church values in its leader? Isn't it the ability to know the whole, to see the connection, to realize the implication, to foster our yearning to grow, to help us to realize all over again that we are loved by God (no matter how big our missionary offering is or isn't!)? In the final analysis, small church people don't want to be bossed around, lorded over, or used as a feather in the cap for a rising star's career hopes. They don't even want to be profitable or efficient. They don't want to sacrifice what is of long-term value for short-term gain nor the good of the

whole to the pushiness of the one. They don't care if they look
wimpy crying at Aunt Florence's funeral. For them to relin-
quish control is to be in control. In short, "nurturing" leadership is the right kind of leadership for the small church—what
the letter writer calls "feminist," what we all have experienced
as "female."

I tip my hat to those male small church pastors who have
matured past "masculine" leadership styles and have served
their people with love, respect, care, and integrity over the
course of the years. But why, I wonder, has the church in large
measure excluded from its leadership the half of the population most likely to provide nurturing leadership? I refer to the
female half. The fact of the matter is that increasingly women
are the ones who will accept a small, rural nonglorious pastorate with barely adequate housing and less than adequate salary. One way our denomination has found to foster the
consideration of female clergy by small churches is to provide
female interim pastors. Many parishes who are not willing to
consider accepting female applicants will agree to a female
interim because one is available "now" an "it won't last forever." Then, once the congregation experiences the quality of
caring leadership in their interim, their eyes are opened for the
possibilities of a woman as a pastor. (The Catch-22 in our
denomination is a "rule" against endorsing an interim for the
pastorate in that congregation.)

Some would consider me unconscionable for advocating
that female pastors accept small church pastorates at substand-
ard wages. I agree. It is inequitable. But would you say the
cause of Christ is being served when a church that is offering a
pastor as much as it can goes pastorless while a woman called
by her God to serve God's people waits for months and years
for an "equitable" position to open up?

Career Change

Situation One. There are in my "wider" parish two men who
are dealing with career changes. Both have been successful
middle-level businessmen. Both are highly gifted in working

with people. Both have high spiritual perception and motivation. Both found the corporate world to be less than fully spiritually rewarding. Both have adequate pension programs
and/or investments to keep from going hungry. Both are looking for "something meaningful" to do for the rest of their active
days. And in spite of their corporate backgrounds, both would
make excellent small church pastors!

Situation Two. A seminary professor once told me that he
believed the Spirit of God was no respecter of persons, that the
Holy Spirit moved in ways that gave no consideration to race,
color, age, or wealth. God, he claimed, is the ultimate equal
opportunity employer. But why the Holy Spirit has been so
active of late in calling a disproportionately huge number of
white, middle-class, suburban women into theological studies,
he had no idea! Whether he saw this as good, bad, or indiffer-
ent, I couldn't determine. But for the small church it may in
fact be a godsend.

For both of these groups of people, meaning is much more at
issue than money. While it is not always easy for an individual
small church to recruit such a person, the church as a whole,
coordinating with seminaries and denominational structures,
could be gainfully employed in recruiting "second career" people and making constructive matches between them and many
small churches.

The Retired Pastors

The pastor old enough but too poor to retire who continues
to minister in a less demanding church setting is a tried and
true approach to filling the small church pastorate. Not much
more need be said except to offer a few brief comments. One:
The same demographic trend that will result in fewer clergy
available in the next decade will also result in a surfeit of
retired clergy. Many of these will be too wise, capable, and still
energetic to be let out to pasture. What may be a loss for the
church at large may well be a boon for the small church. Two:
We may well see more creative approaches to the involvement
of retired clergy in the years ahead. For example, the American

Baptists have had a Ministers-at-Large (MAL) program for a number of years. Retired pastors who apply are screened and assigned an MAL position—primarily interim ministry. These positions are short—usually less then eighteen months—and are located all over the country. The MAL office makes the matches, and the MAL pastor (and spouse) is off on an all-expense-paid ministry trip to a new part of the country. MAL is not a permanent, long-range solution to financing the small church pastorate, but it is an example of what can be done. Three: Reverend W. Stanley Pratt, the pastor who preceded me on Block Island, came to pastor in a preretirement situation. He was paid half of our denomination's minimum at that time, but was given freedom to pursue other income opportunities. (Once I made the mistake of referring to him as a part-time minister. Our treasurer reminded me in no uncertain terms that he was not considered part-time. He was full-time. Whatever time the church didn't need, he could fill with his own interests!) During his six-year tenure, he worked with the church leaders in adopting a more functional set of bylaws, worked with the Episcopal Mission on establishing an Ecumenical Church School, brought many "fringe" people into full membership, and generally enlarged the functioning and vision of the congregation. On his retirement the church called and financed the first full-salaried (at the denomination's minimum level) pastor in three decades! Through his retirement the church ministry got renewed energy and vision!

The Next-Best Thing

From the Administrative Point of View

If a church cannot obtain the services of its own full-time trained clergy, what then? What is the next-best thing? The answer depends upon whom you ask. If you ask someone in the denominational structure, you are very likely to get a bureaucratic response. This is based upon the position that the clergy are the significant variable in the equation. After all, the clergy are trained professionals and, more importantly, they are in the system. The bureaucracy directly or indirectly places them, makes the churches pay their pensions and health insurance, and offers them the hope of "advancement." The denomination sees the clergy, not the churches, as the primary reality. So it tends to organize around the clergy class.

Yet churches are a rather permanent part of the landscape no matter how they are perceived "from above." Churches can exist with benign denominational neglect for years. They can survive denominational hosility. (One of my colleagues is a supply minister for a small church in Pennsylvania. This church was closed by its denomination and the members directed to join a larger church across the river. They didn't. They waited twenty years for a new denominational regime to come to power. They applied to reopen. They received permission. They are still small, but they have proved they were too strong to kill. My friend chuckles at how that congregation made the denomination eat crow. Of course, hostility is not the only kind of relation between the denomination and small churches. The point is that the denomination-small church relation is not the most crucial one for the small church.) The clergy, on the other hand, are more highly dependent on the denominational structure and are perceived as the organizing focus when viewed from above.

So the second-best preference from an administrative point of view is to shape church configuration to the pastor's economic requirements and workload schedule.

From the Point of View of the Small Church

The small church person, on the other hand, sees things very differently. The pastor is not so much valued as a member of a class (clergy), although that is usually deemed a prerequisite. The pastor is valued as a member of a group—us, this church, this family of faith. To the degree that he or she is one of us, to that degree is he or she significant to our life, for our life together is what is important. The organizing focus for the local lay person is "my church," not the pastor's workload. Sure it is important, but it is secondary.

This should not be surprising. It can be deduced quite readily if one accepts the conceptual model put forward in Chapter 3. First of all, parishes are not likely to see each other as allies, as entities similar enough to merit lumping together. From an administrative point of view, it may seem that two parishes of one denomination in close geographic proximity are redundant. But the reason they exist in the first place is because they are not redundant. Not to the people in them. Each claims a different patriach—or, at least, to be the only true descendant of their founder! Each resonates to a different heritage. Each embodies a different culture. Merging parishes, which seems so straightforward from the administrative point of view, is in fact an enterprise on the order of uniting the Hatfields and the McCoys. Even yoking is difficult, because (and this is the second point) there is something wrong about sharing leaders in the folk mentality. As a child I knew my dad was not perfect (apparently an inherited trait!), but I also knew that he was *my* dad. He didn't give us Monday through Wednesday and then spend Thursday to Saturday with another family in the next village. Imagine the psychotherapy I would need if he had. Or imagine two tribes in, say, Africa. One is warfaring, the other peace loving. Or one is agricultural, the other organized around the hunt. Or one is coastal and seafaring, the other inland and landlubbing. Or one claims descent from the sun, the other the moon. Now imagine a fellow showing up and setting himself up as chief *of both tribes.* If they have their druthers, the tribesmen (of both tribes) will not accept this arrangement. If they have to accept it, it won't be a happy marriage.

Yet, you say, yoked parishes do work; I know plenty of situations where things are working out OK. True enough. But ask any yoked parish if they would prefer their own clergyman if it could be arranged. I'm guessing in over 90 percent of the cases the answer would be yes! So the question is how.

Second Preference: Our Own, Trained, Part-Time Clergy

The bivocational pastor is another tried-and-true "solution" to the small church clergy "problem." From bus drivers to fund-raisers, from carpenters to psychoanalysts, from Peter and Paul to today, from Jerusalem to Alaska, supporting oneself from employment other than the pastoring of a congregation is a functional way to make pastoral ministry happen. It would be overstating to say that the full-time "kept" clergy is an aberration, but it might be healthy in a compensating sort of way to say just that, in light of the low esteem in which bivocational ministry is held today.

The Southern Baptist Convention in a recent attempt to project the economies of their desired church growth concluded that the vast majority of all their hoped-for new churches would of necessity have bivocational pastors. Maybe that was not their original idea, but now the bivocational pastorate is central to their hopes for the future. How central is the bivocational structure to our thinking about the small church? Maybe it is time we made it more central, more legitimate, and built the structures necessary to support and expand it.

There is nothing magical about each denomination's minimum pastoral salary figure. But it does constitute a benchmark. Unfortunately, it is often used in the same way in which pass-fail grading in some of my college courses was used. Those who do not pass, fail. Those who surpass the minimum number by a goodly amount have Lady Luck with them in the Pastoral Lottery. Those who equal or pass the minimum are still in the game. Those whose best salary package is below the minimum are relegated to Limbo Land, some never to be heard from again.

At the same time, I hear colleagues express guilt over time "stolen" from their parishes in order to pursue other areas of challenge. I see others locked into base-level situations that are becoming increasingly marginal as their families grow. I see others who could use one or two days a week of outside income, but who shy away from retreating into a part-time position. Wouldn't it be more honest and helpful for congregations to make a fraction—with their package as the numerator and the denomination's minimum as the denominator? The resulting fraction would be the percentage of the pastor's work time the parish feels entitled to. Or to put it another way, the difference would be the amount of his or her working time that the pastor feels can be given to other pursuits. There are many benefits to the congregation from this approach. It is more honest and will tend to keep the pastor and the congregation happier since there is a feeling of equity on both sides. Second, it will help by freeing time and legitimating the pastor's efforts to supplement his or her income. Third, it will encourage the pastor to better time management. Frequent are the times I get as much done in two days as I would in three days if I know I have a commitment for that third day. Fourth, it keeps the pastor from getting stale. The outside involvement can have a balancing or catalytic effect that rebounds to the congregation's well-being.

The basic approach can be carried one step further. If a congregation wants to reward the pastor's performance with a pay increase but can't afford all that it would like, the fraction can be invoked again. This time the numerator is the offered package, while the denominator is increased by the amount that should be added due to increases in experience and the cost of living and other factors (most denomimations have tables for calculating these increases). Effectively, then, the pastor is given some additional discretionary time. This communicates to the pastor both the congregation's appreciation and their OK to earn more outside income. And it will likely result in little loss to the congregation, as the pastor (assuming basic competence and the capacity to grow) is one year wiser and more efficient. (A variation on this theme is an arrangement offered to a colleague by his small church in Connecticut. Wanting to give him a raise, but lacking the funds, they increased his vacation time. He was pleased with their thoughtfulness, and his family appreciated the additional time together). OK, fine, but what to do with the one or one and a half or two days a week the parish has freed up the pastor? Is every would-be small church pastor on his or her own, or is there something we can do corporately?

A major missions conference of our denomination was held in Ocean Park, Maine, a number of years ago, and I addressed the assembly on mission and the small church. After the talk I fielded questions. One person asked what the denomination could do to help the small church pastor financially. Plowing in where angels fear to tread, I answered, "There are two problems. One is financing the small church pastor. The second is keeping what's done regionally and nationally on target with the local situation. Right now some competent local pastors take regional or national denominational positions. Over time even the best may lose touch with their local church roots. They get regionalized or nationalized. Then may begin to think that what flies at headquarters will fly in the local church. We could solve both problems with one fell swoop. We could chop up the duties and the pay of a lot of these jobs into their component pieces. Divide these out among the competent and needy local pastors. And just keep one megalomaniac workaholic type at headquarters to coordinate it all." Well, everybody chuckled and the idea was promptly lost at sea. And since it would be an administrative nightmare anyway, why bother?

Why bother, that is, until the denomination starts running in the red! In a cost-saving move, the American Baptist Churches of Connecticut have replaced a statewide staff position with four part-time positions. Each of the part-time positions is filled by a local pastor, three of them small church pastors. The additional income is a help to each; the challenge of the position, the recognition, the collegial and staff relationships—these all add up to something significant. This kind of move cannot and should not be replicated everywhere, but it is a model that bears watching and wider trial.

Third Preference: A Shared, Part-Time, Trained Clergy

This is basically the option of yoked parishes or multipoint

parishes. This is an age-old structure, also. It has worked well
in many situations. In the previous debate section, I have
described some liabilities regarding it. A more thorough
description of its possibilities, as well as other advantages of
cooperative ministry, is to be found in *Cooperative Ministry:
Hope for Small Churches* by Marshall E. Schirer and Mary
Ann Forehand.[3]

A wrinkle in this approach, which may well merit special
attention because of its particular possibilities in suburban and
exurban areas, is the cluster ministry concept. This concept,
developed by David Brown, first in northeastern Vermont and
currently in central Connecticut, advocates a team and staff
approach to the paid ministry in the context of a number of
small churches. The concept is intricate and requires a skilled
administrator. Simplified, it goes something like this. Five
small churches, for example, in one general geographic area
join together in a cluster. On an average each could afford
about four-fifths of a full-time clergy. Together they can hire
four full-time people. The four would be constituted similarly
to the staff of a large church, selected for their functional spe-
cialties (for example, administration, music, youth work,
counseling, and so forth). The officiating/preaching is divided
up in such a way that each parish can get to know each of the
staff over time. Each congregation is responsible for its own
building and "buys" pastoral ministry from the cluster. While
this approach does not eliminate all of the concerns raised previously in the "debate," it might alleviate them by diffusing the
whole issue. And this may be an advantage for suburban and
exurban people who may prefer multiple functional competence to a folksy generalist and whose commitment to place
and people is understood primarily in terms of benefit rather
than identity.

Fourth Preference: Lay Leadership

It is unfortunate when a small church that cannot obtain a
trained clergy man or woman feels they therefore cannot have
a pastor. I often wonder how many lay people the Lord calls to
minister to his small churches who never hear or act on the call

because they are wearing "clergy blinders"—seeing only clergy as pastors. Our God calls lay people to be pastors, too! And consider the advantages. Usually the lay person is already there. He or she knows the people and loves the congregation. Often his or her financial needs are within the congregation's ability to meet. And though perhaps less well versed in systematic theology, he or she will probably have a natural sense of what will fly and how to deal with these particular folk. My own parish acknowledges the two-decade-plus tenure of Deacon Thomas Dodge as pastor. He was a godly man and well loved. He more ably served the congregation than the two trained clergy who preceded him, both of whom left behind a legacy of hurt feelings and bruised relationships!

One approach to lay pastoring is the raising up of lay people already within the parish. This is most effective when conceived as a team ministry. In fact, the Episcopal Church has a program for rural and remote parishes designed to move them toward leadership self-sufficiency called TEAM (Teach Each A Ministry). Apparently pioneered by Rev. William Gordon, former bishop of Alaska, and applied by Rev. Wosley Frensdorff, bishop of Nevada, TEAM seeks to lift up the lay people already in their parishes to handle their own affairs, including worship, whether or not a priest is present. In Pioche, Nevada, the TEAM concept got an early trial. The congregation of 31 in a town of 680 (these mostly Mormons) decided that they needed a warden, a secretary, a treasurer, a women's group president, a Sunday School supervisor, and a priest to function as a church. By calling, coercion, and concensus, the lay people filled each function—including priest! Mrs. Jean Orr, who years earlier, as a teenager, had felt a calling to the pastoral ministry, felt a renewed call. This was confirmed by the congregation, and after her training Mrs. Orr became an ordained Episcopalian priest. Now Jean contributes her gift to her small church, officiating at worship and contributing to the entire team ministry.

In a little town on the western edge of Vermont sits a brick Methodist Church. It had been built a century or so ago. Since then the congregation has had its ups and downs. Most recently downs. A few years back they had been able to obtain an ordained clergyman right out of seminary, but the match had not been made in heaven. The few dozen who welcomed him to their pulpit eventually dwindled down to half a dozen. Their income nosedived, too. Then their pastor was reassigned, and the church was left without people, pastor, or pence. What to do? Finally, the bishop assigned a lay minister. Methodist Lay Ministers are usually recent retirees who, desiring to pastor, have been given basic and pragmatic training and assigned to parishes. They do course work by correspondence fall and spring and on campus in the summer. They are not accorded ordained status, but they sure do minister! This particular lay minister, frail to look at, soft-spoken, self-effacing, being paid a pittance, living primarily off his pension, just started loving the people. Slowly, they started trickling back in. By the time I got to visit, the enthusiasm in the congregation was so thick you needed a knife to cut it. Attendance was up to what it was three years ago and then some. Giving was up. Energy was up.

"We're doing our roast beef suppers again. They've got it down to a science, and you'd better not get in their way," the not-Rev. said with a warm smile.

"Yep, and we're even feeding some of the folk from the home. Fifty came to our last supper!" said a member.

"Fifty?" I said.

"Fifty!" he repeated. "Some of our members didn't want to let 'em in unless they paid. But I jus' sent them right on in. Why not? It's the right thing to do. Isn't it, Rev.?"

The not-Rev. just kept on smiling, beaming actually. Beaming at his flock, renewed in ministry, vision, and energy.

So now you know why I'm not convinced about the sequence of these preferences. I think maybe I've saved the best for last!

Well, enough said about paying the pastor. Let's get on to something really important, like the church building.

6

Tacking into the Wind

Maintaining the Church Building

"I think it's great that Jesus Christ is our sure Foundation, but how are we going to fix the leak in our roof?"

"Did Gladys really say that?" I asked my wife incredulously. She had just returned from the ladies' group meeting of the parish to which I'd just come to pastor a few months previously.

"Yes. But don't take it personally. That is just how she thinks."

"And I thought she liked me," I said defensively, overreacting, feeling all those bad things I was mature enough to recognize as immature, but not mature enough to avoid.

"She does like you. But remember she's ninety. She's seen two church buildings burn down and about a dozen pastors come and go. So that's why she said what she did about the money."

"Yeah, but 'Skip the raise for the pastor. Who knows how long he'll last, but we gotta take care of this building. So give the money to the trustees.' Geez!"

"So prove her wrong. Last longer than the building. When you're as old as this church and your arches still haven't fallen, then you can take it personally."

"I should have taken my father's advice and become a dentist. People open their mouths all they want, but they don't say anything hurtful when you've got the drill in your hand."

How many of the church's dollars are eaten up by building maintenance may make a crucial difference in the physical well-being and mental attitude of the pastor. As matters of pride and good stewardship, efficient and adequate care of the properties of the church are important to church members, too. What can be done? Let us consider three approaches to the issue of financing church building maintenance. These are (1) reducing costs, (2) raising money and/or resources, and (3) other avenues.

Reducing Costs

There are basically two approaches to reducing the cost of using and maintaining a building. One is to reduce the use on the basis that wear and tear and utility costs are in proportion to use. The second is to reduce the costliness per use.

Reduce the Use

The knee-jerk reaction to red ink is to cut back on expenses. Use the building less and it will cost less. Of course, the least expensive option is to not use the building at all. Or sell the building. Invest the funds and the church will be in the black every year. Carried to this extreme we see what is wrong with this approach. The strength of any church and its hope for the future is the quality and faithfulness of its social functioning— the church gathered to worship, fellowship, learn, and serve. Cut back on gathering and you weaken your strength and diminish your future. Yet there are some ways to reshape the patterns of building use.

One is to consolidate meetings. For example, if the youth group meets Wednesday evenings at 6, the choir Mondays at 7, and the Trustees Tuesdays at 8, moving all of these meetings to the same evening would reduce midweek heating (or cooling) costs by as much as two-thirds. A second pattern is to migrate seasonally. For many winters our congregation worshiped in Fellowship Hall. After Christmas, the men would move our electric organ out of the sanctuary and shut off the radiators. Just before Easter, back we went. We didn't like it, but it helped to get us through some lean years. A congregation which is family-sized or which has a one-room church building may consider worshiping in homes for the winter. It may not feel like church, but outreach might jump significantly. Many people who wouldn't consider going cold turkey into a church building would attend a service at a friend's house. A third pattern is to mix both types of models—worship and large group meetings in the church building and board meetings, Bible studies, and other small group meetings in the homes of parishioners. The pearl in the oyster of home meetings is the different feel of the shared experience and the shift in the quality of interaction. It is not by accident that many revivals have been greatly furthered by home meetings, cottage prayer meetings, or base community groups.

Reduce the Costliness Per Use

Here we are dealing with making the church facility more efficient. The first thing to check is heat loss. Is the building insulated? Are the windows glazed with thermopane or covered with storm windows? Are the doors tight to the weather? Is there an airlock at each entrance? Most denominations, state energy offices, utility companies, or even some local contractors will perform an energy audit at no or low cost. While such an audit may result in a laundry list of improvements too lengthy for most small churches to handle at once, it will provide a long-range battle plan for reducing building use costs.

Financing improvements is not as intimidating as it may appear at first. Many denominations offer low-interest loans for energy improvements. Certain parishioners or friends of the church who may not be willing to make a major financial donation to this cause may very well be willing to loan the church monies below the bank's rate of interest. And many churches will find that the rate of return on their invested funds is greater if put into efficiency improvements than if kept in an average certificate of deposit.

A second area to consider is how efficiently the utility needs are being met. Is the furnace efficient and operating smoothly? Is the heat zoned so that only the areas in use get heated? Is the most cost-effective fuel being used for the church's situation and purposes? Is the lighting switched so that only the area in use is illuminated? Are outdoor lighting switches on timers? Are there fans on high ceilings to push the hot air back down?

A third area concerns patterns of use. What are the functions that are important to your style of church? Its worship? Its Sunday School? Its fellowship? What else? How do you like to live out these functions? What spatial arrangements would best serve your approach? I visited a church in New Jersey with a cozy and spacious chapel-like sanctuary. The comfortable feeling it afforded intrigued me. The pastor explained that the sanctuary had been remodeled. Its original cathedral-like proportions were no longer appropriate to the size of the present congregation. In addition to a savings on utilities, the change had a profound and positive impact on the morale of the congregation.

A church with a dozen graded classrooms may find its present size and attitude better reflected in a one-room, open classroom Sunday School setting. I read recently of a shrinking Baptist church with a huge sanctuary entering into a deal with a rapidly growing Nazarene church with a smallish church building. The two congregations realized they would fit better in each other's building. So they swapped! Spatial use patterns that are meaningful and functional should, of course, be respected. But when a change in the function and/or preferences of the church has occurred, space can sometimes be reshaped to create greater efficiency.

Raising Money and/or Resources

The way to keep the church doors open is not to close the doors! Reducing costs is not the only way to meet the costs of maintaining the church building. Another way is to open the doors—to use the church building as a source of income. I am not suggesting placing a "For Rent" ad in the classifieds, but

~eeping an open mind and an open door to some needs in the community. In our town, two nonprofit groups needed a place to hold committee and public meetings. "Welcome," our church said. Our historical society needed an auditorium to offer a series of presentations. "Look no further," our church said. The local food co-op thought our Fellowship Hall would be a great place from which to make their monthly food distribution. "Come on down," we said. Our local AA and Al-Anon groups needed a place to meet, brew coffee, and store their literature. "Use our 'Grandma's Kitchen,'" we said. These groups, along with the school, musical groups, wedding parties, a forming synagogue, mainland retreat groups, and others regularly use our church building. And though we don't charge rent, we will receive nearly three thousand dollars in "thank yous" this year. And that goes a long way toward our utility and maintenance costs!

A second way of using the building to care for itself is also demonstrated by our congregation. Fifteen years ago the town needed a place to house a drop-in center. Such a "ministry" was badly needed in our community. Our church did not have personnel or budget to contribute, but we did have space. "Take our basement," we said. So out of our basement for a decade and a half the town has run a recreation center, now also including a pre-school program. For this space we have received no rent whatsoever (only reimbursement for electrical usage). So what help is that, you ask? Well, when the recreation center program moved in, the basement was a basement. They added a bathroom, kitchen area, darkroom, furnace, and heating system. They have remodeled and improved the space to meet fire code requirements. They have replaced the old doors with thermally efficient ones and paid a proportion of the fire alarm system and the cost of a cement stairway. And they heat the basement all winter, making it a lot easier to heat our sanctuary and Fellowship Hall. And considering that we would have to heat the basement to keep our pipes from freezing were the recreation center not there, we do gain from their presence.

Other Avenues

Here are some miscellaneous thoughts on other approaches to keep up with building maintenance.

Force the Pride Issue

For years I had been disgusted with the state of our balcony. The tiers were uneven, the seating random. Junk and debris was attracted to it as if by magic. Occasionally the trustees would make a halfhearted effort at improvement, only to retreat quickly, licking their wounds. Ugh, but what to do? Meanwhile, all the men in the church were following the exploits of the New England Patriots. Their new head coach, Raymond Berry, had them playing great ball, but, more importantly, he had brought a much needed calmness, respect, and integrity. Later I found out he was a dedicated and out-spoken Christian man. After the Superbowl, I wrote to him, inviting him to share his faith from our pulpit. Was I shocked when he accepted! Working with the deacons and trustees, we prepared for his coming. The trustees figured we'd have quite a crowd. "What if we need to put people in the balcony?" I asked innocently.

"Boy, we'd better do something about that," they figured. Planes, wood, saws, and nails materialized, and the balcony was set to rights once and for all. And sure enough, "Berry's Bleachers" were full that Sunday! And our trustees were proud.

But Don't Be Too Proud

Frequently other churches have men's and ladies' groups, seniors or youth groups with manual skills and a desire to help other parishes. A mission church not too far away from me hosts a camping group each spring specifically to repair and upgrade their one-room church. This group has done things— painting the whole building and installing a handicap access ramp—that the elderly congregation could never do alone. It is a nice example of the body of Christ caring for its own. But, of course, they had to ask or say yes or acknowledge this need. Humble, but effective.

Figure Out What's Going for You

People like to vacation on our island. Churches used to call asking us to let their youth group "camp out" in our Fellowship Hall. "Sure," I said, "and while you are here, how's 'bout helping us out, too?"

For years we had young people painting this, moving that, cleaning here, repairing there. We've outgrown this arrangement now, but in the early years of my pastorate it was a big help. What's going for you? Inner-city parishes could host country youth groups. Country parishes could host inner-city groups. Churches with lots of history might find some support from historical societies, and so forth.

There Is an Elephant of Fun in Every Job

That's how my children misquote a line from one of their favorite movies. But they are right. Find the element of fun, and work becomes joy. Where is the fun in maintaining the church building? For us it's in the fellowship. We don't overdo our work days, to be sure; but when we get together to clean, or repair, seal the driveway, or refinish the Communion table, we enjoy it! The sharing, the camaraderie, and the sense of a job (well) done make it fun, not work—and saves us money, too.

7

Setting the Course

Doing Christ's Mission: Low Budget—High Impact

Mission Understandings

"Mission. The denomination is always talking about mission giving. And rightly so. I mean, our missionaries and relief programs are good . . . and right to do. But when we are always in the red, how are we going to find money to give to mission?"

Part of the problem in doing mission in the small church is the idea that mission is something that we finance and others do. So if we are short on finances, we can't do mission. Nothing could be further from the truth. Mission can be done with money or without it. The lack of money does not need to be the end of our mission. Financial resources allow certain types of mission, true. But not all of mission is of this type. Let us reconsider our understanding of mission.

A while back I wrote an article on mission in *The Five Stones*, a newsletter for small churches. In it I defined mission as "participating with God in the transformation of human life—individual, corporate, and institutional."[1] This understanding presupposes God's activity in the human arena. It invites us to join forces with the divine in a cause of eternal consequences. It sees the multilevel reality of human life as the end of the missionary enterprise. It implies the transformation mentioned in Romans 12:1-2.

I appeal to you therefore, brethren, by the mercies of God, to present your bodies as a living sacrifice, holy and acceptable to God, which is your spiritual worship. Do not be conformed to this world but be transformed by the renewal of your mind, that you may prove what is the will of God, what is good and acceptable and perfect.

Mission of this type is focused on the who (missioners and missionees) and the where (where is the transformation leading?). The how (dollars and programs) is a necessary but entirely subordinate issue. Further, I claimed that mission activity occurs on four levels. These four I have labeled **presence, people, pattern** and **program.**

The first level of mission is mission as **presence.** By this I simply mean that the mere presence of the church in a community is a ministry. This ministry has many facets. The first is symbolic. It has been said that the church was deliberately placed in the center of virtually every New England village and deliberately constructed with its spire pointing heavenward so that it would stand as a continual reminder of the God/human connection. I was shocked into silence one day while chatting on the street corner with a townsperson who has never ever worshiped in our church. She said, "You know I don't go to church. But still it is very important to me to know that it is there. Just its being there kind of anchors things."

The second facet of the ministry of presence is psychological. Carl Burke told me the story of an encounter he had with an elderly lady in Appalachia. He rocked a while with her on her front porch. In answer to his questions she shared the ups and downs of her life.

"Can't anybody improve the situation?" Carl asked.

"Well, the university people. They tried. They did a whole lot for nine months. Then they left, and we ain't seen hide nor hair of them since. Then the government folk set up some programs. They lasted 'least a year and a half. Now they're gone, too. I s'pose they did a little good while it lasted. But things went right back or even worse."

"Hopeless, huh?"

"No. There's one thing that gives me hope, Mr. Burke." She pointed across the hollow to a small, paint-peeling, rickety-looking little church. "That's what gives me hope. It's always there. Always helping. Always lifting me up."

The third facet of the ministry of presence is pragmatic. The church building itself is a great tool for ministry. Lots of good things happen outdoors or downtown. Lots of good things can happen in homes or school. But lots of good things have no place to call home. I have already shared how our church houses a food co-op, AA, Al-Anon and ACOA (Adult Children of Alcoholics) meetings, the Historical Society, and economic development groups. There are also youth group retreats, school concerts, arts and crafts exhibitions, just to mention a few. This open-door policy of our church is our deliberate mission stance. This is a ministry option or potential option for your church, too, and it doesn't take many dollars to do.

The second level of mission is the mission of **people**. This is the most significant level of mission for the small church, I believe. It is the kind of mission that flows from its nature and the kind of mission that is its strength. It is quite simply the ministry of people to people, the caring that makes us human and that Christianizes our social environment.

People relating to people is the guts of the small church, and derivatively, the small church's mission. For when, in faith and obedience, our personhood admits the presence of God's living and loving Spirit, real person-to-person mission takes place. When the donor of memorial flowers drops them by a shut-in's house after church, that is mission. When our church treasurer knits a sweater for a soon-to-be-born baby of an unwed young woman in town, she is engaged in mission to those who people her world. When one of our trustees drives a blind neighbor to a seniors luncheon, that is mission. The number and quality and diversity and depth of personal relations—people connections—constitute a natural mission of the small church.

Now an interesting thing about this kind of mission is its budget. It doesn't have one. Not one to speak of anyhow. How much does it cost to drop off flowers after church or purchase a couple of skeins of yarn or pick up someone on your way or pour a second cup of coffee or walk an extra mile? Only a little caring. And while caring can't be created by the pastor or elders or mission committee, it can be nurtured. Connections can be pointed out to people; even a single act of reaching out can be encouraged; and all ministry can be rewarded with recognition and praise, until people mission becomes a ministry habit.

The third level of mission in the small church is the mission of being a **pattern**. A pattern of what? A pattern of a more righteous and healthy lifestyle. Pause a minute and list what's wrong with our society. What are the elements of our national lifestyle that are out of sync with the biblical picture?

Our lists will vary, of course, but my hunch is that there will be four problems on each of our lists:

1. We are a consumptive, wasteful, and inefficient society. We have reduced the spiritual level to the material and, finding this unsatisfying, must devour ever-increasing amounts of things in an unreachable quest for fulfillment.

2. We are an impersonal people. Millions don't know their neighbors' names, never mind their needs, their hopes, their struggles. We have reduced pretty women to titillating objects and children to consumption sinks. Men, who mistakenly thought they were the beneficiaries of our economic system, find, rather, that they are used up by it. We have become afraid to be persons, afraid of our own humanity.

3. We are socially adrift. It is not only that we don't have any compelling national goals, except maybe to dig ourselves an even deeper materialistic hole. It is also that we have no moorings. We no longer know from whence we've come. We are no longer rooted to the soil, to the village, to a social structure, to a life-orienting world view. Even rural people think that what's going on in Washington, DC, or New York or Los Angeles is more important than what is going on next door or in the village or the county seat. In seeking to be cosmopolitan and universal, we have become disoriented and homogenized.

4. We are atomized, too! It's every man, woman, and child for himself or herself. We used to talk about the family unit as if it were an enduring reality. Today it is so ephemeral and so multiform that we can only talk meaningfully about its components, the individual. We are a country greatly interested in freedom, but we have come to believe that freedom is freedom *from*—freedom from obligation, freedom from constricting duty, freedom from the demands of others. Only the isolated individual is free from these things—free to be alone and empty.

In the face of these pathologies of our society stands the small church! The small church embodies the pattern of a different way of living.

1. In the face of consumption, the small church is, I daresay, the most efficient organization around. Look at all the worship, service, fellowship, and learning that goes on in the small church. Divide this by the total budget, and you come up with an incredible benefit-cost ratio. The small church knows how to squeeze six cents of value out of every nickel. And if they don't have the nickel, they make do anyhow. Yes, the small church lives on the margin, but it knows how to make its resources stretch and stretch and stretch.

2. In the face of the impersonalness of our society, in the small church you are known by name. It might be a nickname you are not proud of! ("Yesterday Tony 'Too Tall' Pappas pitched our softball team to victory." I'm five-feet-four-inches short. The turkeys on the other team tried to rattle me by rubbing it in. But that's OK. I've just nicknamed *them* "Whiff.") In the small church everyone is known personally. Everyone has a place. Everyone is somebody (hopefully, on their way to being somebody better, but nobody is a nobody).

3. In the face of homogenized living, the small church is refreshingly local, rooted, parochial, and idiosyncratic.

Imagine what a loss it wold be if every snowflake was on a quest to become generic. The beauty of the small church is its individuality, its color, its character, its history, its ways. Absolutely unique. And even if it is myopic and inbred, it is still more healthy in form than being homogenized.

4. In the face of isolation and atomization, the small church is bonding together. Small churches are starting to realize and live out the truth that no matter how small the twigs, there is strength in the bundle. Newsletters, books, conferences, and revitalization of local groupings are starting to demonstrate in and of themselves the power of grassroots connectedness.

In all these ways the small church performs the ministry of being leaven in society. To the degree that it lives out its nature, it has a mission to a society gone awry.

The fourth level of mission is the mission of **programs**. This is the explicit organizing of resources to meet needs. Mission promotions and collections are in this category, as are soup kitchens, day-care centers, halfway houses, senior luncheons, and emergency shelters. Anything that through administration applies resources to need is an example of programmatic mission.

Let's say a few things about this type of mission before we list a few pump primers. One: There is nothing wrong with this level of mission. The person who sees a thirsty stranger, grabs a cup, persuades the watercooler to share some water, finds someone to deliver the full cup *is* ministering in Jesus' name. Two: This type of mission is not the totality of mission, as if anything else is not mission. We have just spent a good deal of time trying to make this point. Three: Our present hyper-church accounting system seems to register this kind of mission more than the other three kinds. Four: Do what you can at this level, but in your heart remember that this is only one facet of ministering in Christ's name. Don't fall into the trap of thinking that without megabucks you can't minister in this way. You still can. Here are ideas on how:

Mission Actions

1. A rural church in New England has energetic members who love to garden to excess. From mid-August through Columbus Day these small church gardeners come to church with zucchini, cucumbers, tomatoes, green peppers, squash, and so forth. They pile them up on the chancel, and on each Monday a community-action worker distributes them to the homebound and needy.

Cost: zero. Benefit: great.

2. A small urban church in California has older members who don't feel able to visit homes in their community in the evening. Someone had the idea of saying hi over the phone, anyway. Now each week teams gather in the church for their telephone ministry. They intended to offer a friendly greeting in Christ's name and the name of the church—some low-key evangelism. That happened, but what also happened was unexpected. They discovered that many people in their town have no one to talk to, yet many have problems that need talking over. So the church telephoners have found a significant mission: listening.

Cost: extra phone lines. Benefit: great.

3. A church in Texas has been "greened." An unemployed parishioner agreed to grow vegetables for people in the area who are unemployed or hungry. The church provided the plot, blessed by the pastor! Parishioners, people who wish to garden in exchange for pastoral counseling, and others, keep the broccoli, greens, onions, and squash weeded and healthy. So prolific has the garden grown that the parish has seen God's hand in it. The man who started it all is enjoying his second year at it. The opportunity to give back to others some of what God has blessed him with (he now has a job) is rewarding to him as well as beneficial to the hungry.

Cost: minimal. Benefit: great.

4. A small church in North Carolina learned that there are sixty thousand migrant workers in their state—many in need, such as the three hundred migrant children cared for at a day-care center. What needs? Primarily food and clothing, but also

furniture, toys, linens, toiletries, and so forth. One member of the church personally apprized herself of the situation, arranged for a pre-Christmas party for parishioners and migrants, and persuaded the congregation to take on the task of meeting those needs. And how the parish responded! They started combing their attics, basements, and closets. They encouraged the community at large to help and provided a vehicle for that help. They collected truckload after truckload—totaling twenty so far—of needed items and delivered them to the migrants through the day-care center.

Cost: gasoline for 20 truck trips. Benefit: great.

5. A church in Rhode Island was concerned about the plight of the elderly in the community. The elderly were lonely, isolated at home, apart from their friends. They were not eating properly due to poverty or lack of the desire to prepare good meals for one. They needed a forum to share, learn what's happening, and have a context in which some minimum health care (for example, blood pressure tests) could be obtained.

"Why not start a luncheon?" someone at a Bible study asked.

"How could we?"

The group set out to figure out how. For ten years now the monthly luncheons have gone on. Food is donated by restaurants and parishioners. Prepared by a group of men and women with no official leadership but plenty of pride and elbow grease, thirty to fifty seniors are served. No one is turned away. Everyone, servers and served alike, look forward to it.

Cost: kitchen utilities. Benefit: great.

6. There is a church in Maine that used a whole lot of someone else's money to minister to the needs in its neck of the woods. The area is known for a bit of tourism, a bit of manufacturing, and a whole lot of unemployment. People just couldn't keep a roof over their heads, or if they could, they couldn't keep it from leaking. The pastor of three small, poor, rural churches saw the needs of his own parishioners and those in the community beyond and, along with the pastors of seven

other churches, determined to do something about it. The first thing to do was to believe something could be done—that God had placed the puzzle parts of a solution out there and that if brought together, the solution could be realized. The second thing to do was to find those parts—local churches willing to put a few dollars where their hearts were; support from the regional denominational office; local craftsmen willing to serve for low or no pay; trips to wealthier parishes in other states to explain the problem, share the vision, and invite into a partnership in ministry. From these parishes came funds, but more importantly, work crews—groups of people young and old who could and would swing a hammer, wield a saw, or move a paint brush, and who camp out, cook, and convey themselves in order to minister in Jesus' name. And then there were grants with which to buy materials and pay skilled craftsmen. It takes a lot of administrative skill, or maybe just a lot of tender loving care, to gather up all the pieces and fit them into six or more simultaneous re-hab, winterization, or reconstruction projects. But once the people found the vision, the faith, and the elbow grease, they found the dollars, too!

Cost: time and care. Benefit: great.

7. There is a small church in Wisconsin that is engaged in an amazing ministry to Hmong immigrants. Hmongs are a tribal group from the hill country of Laos. The war in southeast Asia and ethnic hostilities there resulted in the displacement of thousands of Hmongs. Many found themselves in refugee camps in Thailand, and many of these have been able to emigrate to the United States. The pastor of a Baptist church in a small Wisconsin town befriended one Hmong family who for some reason had found its way to his particular village. The Hmong family had attended a church with similar theology in southeast Asia, so they felt at home. Imagine the church's surprise when that one family started welcoming scores and scores of their relatives! But they responded with warm Christian love. First they set up a special Bible study for Hmongs. That led to literacy lessons, counseling, securing of rental apartments, donating food, furniture, and clothing, teaching

home maintenance skills, *and* piano lessons. The church even underwrote medical expenses. Then the church started sponsoring Hmongs who wanted to emigrate but had no relatives. The church provided space for the Hmong Mutual Assistance Association to meet regularly. And this was but the beginning of a decade-long ministry with the Hmongs. I say "with" the Hmongs because the ministry is now truly mutual, with the Hmongs through their music, presence, and energy adding immeasurably to the life of the church.

Cost: some, but who's counting? Benefit: great.

8. What could a small church in Iowa do to further peace between the United States and the Soviet Union? Not much, you say. Well, don't tell them, because they feel they've done something significant, and so do I. The church wanted to "(1) make concrete our concern over the escalating arms race and predictions of global nuclear war; (2) make concrete our determination, as ordinary people, to extend the hand of friendship to ordinary people in the Soviet Union; and (3) have a good time doing a community project together." So what to do? Make a quilt, of course. This would be delivered to a sister city in the Soviet Union as a gesture of friendship. The Friendship Quilt needed thirty-five squares, way more than the number of quilters in the church, so the whole town was invited. Thirty-five people signed up for one square each. After coordinating the materials and design, they spent the winter quilting and appliquéing, and then the quilt was done. Off to the Soviet Union it went with a great deal of love, joy, and meaning. Did it cause *glasnost* and the latest treaty signing? Of course not! But it was one impetus from one small church in one small town that when added to many, many others, moved the world.

Cost: supplies. Benefit: great.

9. A small church in upstate New York found that raising money for mission could be lots of fun. Instead of feeling burdened to raise money for mission, they responded creatively and had a blast doing it. Doing what? Let me tell you how they raised money to support their four denominational annual mission offerings. (1) One church couple cooked and served a breakfast. They donated the food and labor and, along with their children, served the meal. Church people paid as at a restaurant, and $140.85 went to Christ's work. (2) One man in the church organized a Walk-a-Thon. Twenty-three people walked six miles, and $812.15 went to work for God's kingdom. (3) To support international mission, pennies were saved, and $46 went to work in the uttermost parts of the earth. (4) The Ladies Group pledged 10 percent of their Candycane Lane Christmas Bazaar, and $350 went to support retired ministers and missionaries. All of this was in addition to their Hunger Meal and Sunday School Home Banks and their regular mission commitments. Be faithful and have fun at the same time. Sounds great to me.

Cost: some daydreaming and elbow grease. Benefit: $2,150.50.

These nine true stories of low-budget, high-impact missions are not offered as models for your setting. Rather, they have been shared to encourage you to become more open to the vast number of possibilities for outreach ministry awaiting your creativity, sensitivity, and faithfulness. No money for mission? Big deal. If you've got a mind for mission and a heart for helping, God will show you a way.

And remember, mission creates its own energy. See a congregation alive and enthusiastic? You can bet they are doing something significant to benefit those around them. See a congregation dull and boring? You can bet their attention is focused on themselves. Mission creates its own energy by giving the ministers a sense of being biblically faithful, of being in the center of God's will. Mission energizes by providing the ministers the spiritual satisfaction of helping others. Mission energizes by creating a sense of the possible. Mission energizes by attracting others to the cause of Christ. Because of this snowball effect, doing mission is often the means of doing mission. Start small and see what God will accomplish in and through you!

8

The Church Budget

Bother or Blessing?

Tiny, named for his huge frame and large muscles, laughed when I asked him how he enjoyed the town meeting the previous evening. A descendant of one of the island's original settlers and a prominent citizen, Tiny has held many public offices. Now during his retirement he is still active on the Republican Town Committee.

"That was some budget, huh? Two million bucks!" I said priming the pump.

"It's some different, I'll tell you that. When I was first on the council, why we'd meet outside the town hall on the steps. Someone would have an old envelope. Another sharpened the point on his carpenter's pencil. And we made up the town's budget for the next year. We were back at work within an hour. You can't do that no more."

"So how'd it work?"

"Pfff! It worked fine. Everybody knew what the town could do and couldn't do. Nobody figured they were going to change the world by snapping their fingers. People did what had to be done. It worked fine. Not like today."

A pencil-scrawled budget on the back of an old envelope at a private and hastily called meeting is not how budgeting is taught in the seminary course on church administration. Yet it may be a lot closer to the way most small churches actually run. To this day I remember vividly a certain trustee meeting during the first year of my pastorate on Block Island. The treasurer gave her report. I did some quick arithmetic (her report being designed to obscure, not reveal, the amount of budgeted but unexpended funds) and found that there was enough money left in the Sunday School budget to buy some children's books. This I proposed to do and asked for a check. She did not immediately get her checkbook out. When I persisted she directed the full force of her countenance upon me.

"Look, the budget is just something written down on paper. It is not real money. Real money is what we have in the bank. If I spent what the budget said, we'd be broke in a minute. If a bill comes in, I pay it. If I don't have the money, I don't pay it. But for God's sake, let's not go adding to the bills." (On whether this last appeal was a swear or a prayer I am still undecided.) This interchange left me wondering about the real money I had obviously wasted paying the tuition on my church administration course.

How are we to understand budgeting then? Is the budget "just something on paper" or is it a guide for our priorities, the financial expression of our ministry goals, a motivator for the church membership to give more? We will address these questions while we look at some of the nuts and bolts of budgeting.

The Expenditures Budget

The simplest form of budgeting is to prepare a listing of projected expenses. This is not too hard an enterprise if you have been around a while and you are not facing any major changes. One simply goes through last year's checkbook or receipts and tallies up the type and amounts of expenditures. This can be quite simple and straightforward if the tallier is a lumper (for example, pastor + building + miscellaneous = total). Or it can be more complicated and intricate if the tallier has a bad case of detail-itis. With this list of categories and last year's totals in each, a guess or an estimate (depending on your point of view) is made for each item and the sum totaled. This total along with the worksheet that created it comprises the budget.

Chart 1
The Expenditures Budget

Items	Last Year	Next Year
Local Mission	$ 300	$ 335
Denominational Mission	100	105
Fuel Oil	998	1050
Electricity	474	550
Insurance	408	450
Pastor	10,000	9600
Pension	1028	1400
Sunday School	188	225
TOTAL	13,496	13,715

The more detailed the budget *and* the more aware the congregation is of upcoming changes (for example, planned increase in the pastor's medical premium) *and* the better the quality of the assumptions made in the process (for example, whether the next winter will be milder or harsher than the last), the more accurate will the budget be to actual expenditures. This is the budgeting process we have used in my parish for many years. We have tuned it until it is in fact a highly accurate predictor of the actual expenses for the upcoming year. There are two problems with it, though.

The first is that it is a mechanism that gives only the illusion of management. I have often come home from an annual budget committee meeting and answered my wife's innocuous, "How did it go?" with "How could it go? An intelligent chimpanzee who knew the inflation rate could come up with the same budget and do it a lot quicker than we did!" My wife's retort that intelligent chimpanzees are hard to find and so God gave me to this parish did little to assuage the frustration of the moment.

And the second problem is: So what? So what if you know how much money you will need to do this year what you did last year? What good is this piece of information? Precious little good unless something is done with it.

Of course, if this budget is duly adopted, something good can be done with it. The treasurer can decline to pay any bill that exceeds the amount in each category. If this occurs before December, it can bring something the church is doing to a screeching halt or give the church a bad credit rating or both. But it will help you to finish the year in the black.

Expenditures Budget: Variation One

In order to obscure these inherent problems, a more sophisticated budget committee will present the upcoming year's budget to the congregation in a three-column format. The first column is the preceeding year's budget. (Of course, this can only be done by churches that budget two years in a row.) The second column is the actual expenditures for the year. (Well now, this brings us to subvariation A: if the budget is presented before the end of the church's fiscal year, an expenditures-to-date column is an insufficient basis from which to project the next full year's expenses, so another column must be added; for simplicity and to avoid the use of jargon, this is called "the projected expenses year end" column.) Whew! Where was I? Oh, yes. The third column is then the projected expenses for the upcoming year or the next year's budget. This variation is good because it allows the whole congregation to see how smart the budget committee was in predicting the actual level of expenses. (If they were.) This format is bad because it allows the whole congregation to see how dumb the budget committee was in mispredicting the actual level of expenses. (If they were.) So you can see why this format is used selectively by budget committees. However, this format is always good in giving the congregation a sense of the movement (at least over two years) of the church's financial situation. Major discrepancies can be noted and dealt with as appropriate.

Chart 2
The Expenditures Budget—Variation One

Items	Last Year		Next Year
	Budgeted	**Actual**	
Local Mission	$ 300	300	$ 335
Denominational Mission	100	100	105
Fuel Oil	1000	998	1050
Electricity	500	474	550
Insurance	400	408	450
Telephone	420	389	420
Pastor	10,000	10,000	10,600
Pension	1000	1028	1100
Medical	400	462	500
Sunday School	200	188	225
Total	14,320	14,347	15,335

Chart 3
The Expenditures Budget—Variation One; Subvariation A
Figures as of 10/31

Items	Last Year			Next Year
	Budgeted	**Expenditures To Date**	**Projected Year End**	
Local Mission	$ 300	250	300	$ 335
Denominational Mission	100	83	100	105
Fuel Oil	1000	664	1000	1050
Electricity	500	393	475	550
Insurance	400	400	400	450
Telephone	420	324	400	420
Pastor	10,000	8333	10,000	10,600
Pension	1000	835	1000	1100
Medical	400	462	462	500
Sunday School	200	157	200	225
Total	14,320	11,901	14,337	15,335

Expenditures Budget: Variation Two

These previous budgetary formats are too simple for some finance committee hot shots. These folk love to include a "What If" element. (If you are like me, you are about ready to ask "What if we tried getting by without all this stuff?") But this isn't the "What If" they are talking about. The What If they are talking about usually adds two more columns and makes things so complex that it has to be done well before year's end, thereby invoking Variation Two, now giving us a total of at least six columns, not to mention scores and scores of categories of expense, "lines," if you prefer to speak jargonese. By now things are so intricate, convoluted, incestuous, and otherwise removed from the way the New Testament works that the treasurer has begun to demand a computer to keep up with it all.

Well, let's get back to business here—the "What If" columns. What If columns got their catchy name when one day someone asked the question, **"What** could we do for God's kingdom **if** we had more money to spend?" And they began to dream. We could give more to missions; we could pay the pastor more (if he works harder); we could pay off our mortgage sooner; we could build a new Sunday School wing; we could make more long-distance phone calls; and we could burn up more fuel oil. Then upon awaking from their dream, they noticed that virtually every item could be put in a category in the existing budget, and so the What If columns were born. What if people were to give 10 percent more money to the church; then we could do that much more for God. Twenty percent more would mean twice that amount for God. With What Ifs there is no end to what God can do.

What Ifs are good to the extent that they can stretch the vision of a congregation's faithfulness. However, they are prone to mislead us into thinking that all that is lacking in the accomplishment of God's purpose is money, when for churches that use the What If budget approach, it could be argued that it is the other way around. It is the lack of faithfulness that causes the lack of money, not the lack of money that causes the lack of faithfulness. The other liability of this approach for small churches is that it assumes that people are motivated to support expanded efforts for the kingdom, when most small churches are primarily motivated to preserve or enhance their well-being.

Chart 4
The Expenditures Budget
Variation Two
Figures as of 10/31

Items		Last Year		Next Year	What If	What If
		Expenditures Projected				
	Budgeted	**to date**	**Year End**		**+50%**	**+100%**
Local Mission	$ 300	250	300	335		
Denominational Mission	100	83	100	105		
Drop-In Center	*	*	*		+1000	+1000
Soup Kitchen	*	*	*		*	+2000
Fuel Oil	1,000	664	1,000	1,050		
Electricity	500	393	475	550		
Insurance	400	400	400	450		
Telephone	420	324	400	420		
Mortgage	*	*	*		+2000	+2000
New SS Wing	*	*	*		*	+3000
Pastor	10,000	8333	10,000	10,600	+1500	+1500
Pension	1,000	835	1,000	1,100	+ 145	+ 145
Medical	400	462	462	500		
Sunday School	200	157	200	225		
Camp Scholarships	*	*	*		+1500	+1500
Part Time DCE	*	*	*			+2160
Total	14,320	11,901	14,337	15,335	21,480	28,640

The Income Budget

All expenditure-based budgets are worthless unless there is some connection to income and/or resources. Often these connections are assumed and tenuous. Sometimes it is in the awareness of the congregation. If the membership knows that expenses will be up a nickel on a dollar this year, they will up their giving a similar amount. I think that this was the logic

behind our church's budgetary process. But I must say that
there has proved to be many a slip between the budget and the
plate! Sometimes the connection is in the treasurer. The treasurer assumes the budget line figures to be the church's autho-
rized ceiling. And so the treasurer stands ready and willing to
pull the plug when the line amount is equalled. Or sometimes
the treasurer assumes that the budget is what we will spend if
dear old Joe dies and leaves the church a million dollars, but in
the meantime, "No way am I spending all that money!"

If churches are going to use budgets, it seems that it would be
more helpful and effective to make the connection between
income and outgo explicit and clear. This is not an easy thing
to do, but sometimes God allows a crisis that makes the connection a subject of consideration. In the last two years my
church's budget has increased 50 percent! This is due primarily
to the incurring of debt service and some whopping utility
increases. The reasons for the increase were fairly well understood in the congregation, but what to do about it was not. It
could no longer be assumed that the mere reporting of an
increased budget would derive an adequate amount of reve-
nues. "What else could we do?" the church started to ask itself.
The trustees have made some progress in reducing some of
these increases as well as turning some space into revenue. The
men's group organized a chicken barbecue. The ladies are sell-
ing handmade crafts and organizing fairs and auctions. And
our executive board, for the first time in three hundred years,
worked up an income budget to help us get a handle on what
has to happen if we are to scratch our way into the black. I
grant that it is rudimentary, and we are still wrestling with its
form and content, but we did it. It has already taught us that
we don't know enough about who gives what and why. It has
allowed us to ask ourselves in which categories were we at
expected capacity and in which was there room for improvement. It has helped us to take the first few steps into what is for
us a new world. Its form is very much like the expenditure
budget, but it organizes income categories. We isolated
pledges, loose plate offerings, mailed-in donations (these three

categories overlap and intertwine), thank yous for use of the building, interest, special offerings, and fund-raisers. Other churches may have other lines, but this is a start along the waterfront.

Chart 5
The Income Budget

Items	Last Year	Next Year
Pledges	$ 5,200	$ 6,035
Plate	2,120	1,900
Donations	500	600
Thank Yous	1,000	1,500
Interest	500	500
Special Offerings	2,000	1,800
Fund-Raisers	3,000	3,000
Total	14,320	15,335

The income budget format may be expanded with the same procedures used in the expenditures budget. Have fun!

My own humble opinion is that the expenditure budget is overrated in the life of the church and that the income budget is underutilized for the church's well-being. Further, I feel that budgets were not inscribed on the two tablets of stone Moses brought down from Mount Sinai. They are tools, and should be used as any tool: in the manner in which they are appropriate and for the purpose of the church's increased well-being and faithfulness. Having unburdened myself, let me now offer some criteria for the use of budgeting in the small church.

On Using Budgets

The merits of a budgetary process are to be assessed situationally, not theologically. Let me offer the following thoughts on when budgeting may be helpful.

Use a budgetary process when things are changing rapidly and the congregation doesn't realize it. By its very nature budgeting demands the keeping of a track record from year to year. The financial implications of changes that are affecting the congregation will become evident in a multi-year comparison. It will usually be even more helpful if the budgetary process is used for both income and outgo. Budgeting can be used, then, to confront reality, to precipitate a crisis, and to increase awareness.

Use a budgetary process when things are changing rapidly and the congregation is at a loss as to how to proceed. The budgeting process itself raises options and demands decisions. Sometimes an objective procedure that allows the members to focus on what is happening can elucidate handles and starting points. I have already shared how an income budget has helped my congregation start to respond to some bad economic news.

Do not use a budgetary process when things are as they have always been. What's the point? Those who need to know numbers will, and the rest understand the situation intuitively. If the situation is truly static internally and externally, just hire an intelligent chimp. Save the energy of the members for more important things.

Use a budgetary process to move the congregation toward ownership of their future. In parishes where a sense of passivity, disenfranchisement, or irresponsibility exists, the budgetary process can be used as a tool toward greater responsibility and ownership. Select a budget committee that represents the congregation or use the whole congregation as the committee. Present the data as decision points. Encourage the congregation to seek God's will and commit themselves to live it out.

Use a budgetary process to widen the power base. If the economic power in your congregation is too narrowly held by a select few who make decisions privately and unilaterally, the introduction of a budgetary process can bring others on board. This introduction usually occurs best after the death of one of the powerful. (Note: Leave the timing in the hands of God. Just be ready.)

Do not use a budgetary process if there are no decisions to be made and everybody agrees on how to make them. If everyone knows what is going on and everyone agrees that they are doing the best they can with what they've got, don't bother with budgeting; get on with doing.

Use a budgetary process to set goals in a non-future-oriented parish. A congregation that is confronted with ministry options but which is unskilled at long-range planning can use the budgetary process as a means of clarifying their future and making decisions.

To my mind, budgets are like salt: they accentuate, but they don't nourish. If budgeting will help your ministry and faithfulness, by all means use it. But don't get carried away with it. Use only what you need.

9

Epilogue

There is no magical way to be successful in life. No magical way to have a good marriage relationship or raise children. And there is no magical way to finance the small church.

Everything worth doing requires effort, concentration, skill, and love. All of life is a struggle. But the struggling can be joyous. I hope the thoughts on the pages of this book opened up some new insights and possibilities in your thinking. But more than that, I hope this book has encouraged you to be joyous in the struggle. Celebrate your small church life and health. Be proud of each victory. Go forth each day to wrest a blessing out of the struggle. And God will be with you.

Notes

Chapter Two

[1]Letter from Camille Bedard, reported in *The Five Stones*, vol. 2, no. 1 (Fall 1984), p. 13.

Chapter Three

[1]Garrison Keillor, *Lake Wobegon Days*, (New York: Viking Penquin, Inc., 1985), pp. 94-97.

[2]Ferdinand Tonnies, *Community and Society*, 1887, trans. & ed. Charles P. Loomis (New York: Harper & Row Publishers, Inc., 1957).

[3]George A. Theodorson and Achilles G. Theodorson, *Modern Dictionary of Sociology* (New York: Thomas Y. Crowell Co., 1969), p. 173.

[4]*Ibid.*, p. 170.

[5]Robert Redfield, "The Folk Society," *The American Journal of Sociology*, vol. 52 (January 1947), pp. 293-308.

[6]Paul S. Minear, *Images of the Church in the New Testament* (Philadelphia: Westminster Press, 1970), pp. 68,70.

[7]Stan D. Gaede, *Belonging: Our Need for Community in Church and Family* (Grand Rapids, Mich.: Zondervan Publishing House, 1985). See especially Chapter 2, "The Problem of Modernity."

[8]John A. Hostetler, *Amish Society*, rev. ed. (Baltimore: Johns Hopkins Press, 1968), pp. 5-6.

[9]Carl S. Dudley, *Unique Dynamics of the Small Church* (Washington, D.C.: The Alban Institute, 1977), pp. 6,9.

Chapter Four

[1]"The Every Member Un-Canvass—A Stewardship Kit for Small Congregations," by Frank Oglesby, is available from the Resource Center for Small Congregations, Box 752, Luling, TX 78648.

[2]An Adventure in Thanks/Giving Resource Kit includes guides, posters, a Sunday School lesson, sermon ideas, and other items. For more information, write:

Director of Stewardship Services, World Mission Support, American Baptist Churches in the U.S.A., P.O. Box 851, Valley Forge, PA 19482-0851.

Chapter Five

[1]Anthony G. Pappas, *Entering the World of the Small Church: A Guide for Leaders* (Washington, D.C.: The Alban Institute, 1988).

[2]Letter from Elinor Artman, *Action-Information Journal (Washington, D.C.: The Alban Institute,* May/June 1988), p. 23.

[3]Marshall E. Schirer and Mary Anne Forehand, *Cooperative Ministry: Hope for Small Churches* (Valley Forge: Judson Press, 1984).

Chapter Seven

[1]Anthony G. Pappas, "Living As Leaven," *The Five Stones,* vol. 3, no. 2 (Spring 1985), p. 8.

Other Titles in the Small Church in Action Series

Christian Education in the Small Church

Donald L. Griggs, Judy McKay Walther. Quality programs on a tight budget is the goal of a holistic approach to education covering all ages and all church activities. Filled with new ideas for tailoring programs to community needs, designing a curriculum, selecting the resources, building relationships between education and worship, equipping leaders, and much more.

0-8170-1103-X

Developing Your Small Church's Potential

Carl S. Dudley, Douglas Alan Walrath. Dynamic possibilities for churches struggling to survive despite dwindling memberships. New ideas for making positive use of community transition, absorbing newcomers into the church family, reshaping the church's image, and developing programs reflecting community needs.

0-8170-1120-X

Activating Leadership in the Small Church

Steve Burt. People-oriented ideas for encouraging members to volunteer, relational skills needed by pastor and leaders, procedures for selecting a pastor, and twelve helpful guidelines for assessing small church ministry, mission, and programming.

0-8170-1099-8